UNDER
GOD'S
WINGS

Miraculous True
Stories of Christian
Faith and Hope

UNDER
GOD'S
WINGS

Candy Chand

Adams Media Corporation
Holbrook, Massachusetts

Published by
Adams Media Corporation
260 Center Street, Holbrook, MA 02343
www.adamsmedia.com

ISBN: 1-58062-428-6

Printed in Canada.

J I H G F E D C B

Library of Congress Cataloging-in-Publication
data available upon request from the publisher.

This publication is designed to provide accurate and authoritative
information with regard to the subject matter covered. It is sold
with the understanding that the publisher is not engaged in ren-
dering legal, accounting, or other professional advice. If legal advice
or other expert assistance is required, the services of a competent
professional person should be sought.

— From a *Declaration of Principles* jointly adopted
by a Committee of the American Bar Association
and a Committee of Publishers and Associations

Cover illustration by Private Collection/
Fredrick C. Czufin/Superstock

This book is available at quantity discounts for bulk purchases.
For information, call 1-800-872-5627

Dedication

To my mother, the late Yolanda Butto,
who always believed I'd be a writer someday.
This one's for you, Mom.

Contents

❧ *vii* ❧

Acknowledgments

A special thanks:

To my husband, Patrick; daughter, Tiffany; son, Nicholas;
and father, Joe Butto, for believing in me.

To family and friends, for your encouragement.

To Barbara Kennedy, for hours of online story feedback.

To Jennifer Basye Sander and Paula Munier Lee,
for giving me the chance of a lifetime.

To those who contributed story ideas, for sharing their
experiences, their hearts, and their miracles with all of us.

*To each of you, for your kindness and support,
I offer my gratitude.*

Introduction

For some, miracles are a rare occurrence, treasured blessings in scriptures of old. For others, miracles are everywhere. They're in God's still, small voice, speaking quietly within our souls. They're in His guidance, as He reaches out to help us in times of need. Yes, miracles are all around, just waiting for us to stop, pay attention, and acknowledge their existence.

Under God's Wings is a collection of true, inspirational stories meant to warm the heart and touch the spirit. While I was researching this book, people came from far and wide to share answers to prayer, hopes and dreams fulfilled in God's perfect timing, and supernatural interventions. As they studied their family history, they found that God had been faithful all along, blessing their loved ones in times of need, watching over each of them in remarkable ways. They learned the secret of those blessings—gratitude and reaching out to others. And so they wanted to reach out and share these miracles with you.

It's my hope that as you read *Under God's Wings* you'll open your heart to the good things in store for you. It's my desire that you'll discover a life filled with wonder, a life filled with miracles that will overwhelm your soul with gratitude and cause you, in turn, to reach out and share with others.

The Miracle on the Doorstep

William Spoonemore's only wish for Christmas was for a brighter New Year. He desired a gift that could exchange life for death, joy for sorrow, and hope for despair. Only a few months before, William had lost his dear wife of more than 50 years. He missed her tremendously and didn't quite know how he'd continue without her. They had been married so long, had become so intertwined in each other's lives, William began to feel that without his wife, he no longer had a purpose.

Nothing had changed when William awakened on that freezing, dark winter morning of January 21, 1999. As usual, he rose early that day, finding himself restless and unable to sleep. Around 6:30 A.M., he wandered into the living room. It was there that William first heard it, a faint, distant cry. Thinking it was the howls from a neighborhood cat, he went to the door to shoo the feline away. A few minutes later, from the quiet of his couch, William heard it again. This time, he stepped outside and took a good look around. William glanced downward and there he was, resembling the tiny Christ child wrapped in swaddling clothes, a newborn baby boy! Wrapped only in a thin towel, his purple legs were kicking wildly, and his cry was pathetic, desperate, and weak. Not quite sure if he was dreaming, William rushed the baby to the warmth of his living room and placed a blanket around him, trying his best to warm the infant's tender, frigid body. William rocked him gently and began to reassure him, "It's OK, little fellow, you're going to be all right now." Amazingly, at the sound of his voice, the crying subsided.

Suddenly, the surreal moment began to take on a hard reality. Who could have left a newborn baby alone this way? Why would anyone abandon him outside, especially in such dangerous weather? William pulled his thoughts together and dialed his daughter's number. Excitedly, he told her he'd found a tiny baby on his doorstep. Karen was shocked and quickly ended their conversation with instructions: "Dad, I'll be right over; hang up the phone and dial 911." William had been so caught up in the dreamlike moment that dialing 911 had not even crossed his mind.

The emergency operator documented the information as he relayed what had just occurred. She told William to remain calm and promised that an ambulance would arrive shortly. Just as she vowed, in what seemed like only moments, the emergency medics knocked at his door. They took the baby's vitals and tried implicitly to hide their fears for his safety. William asked if the baby would be all right. The medical team said that even a few more minutes outside would have meant certain death for this infant. Although they told William they'd do their best, they all knew the baby was so young and fragile—and the air so cold—that only a miracle could protect him. Only a miracle could preserve his young life.

As the ambulance transported the baby to the hospital, William began to pray. He thanked God for placing the baby safely on his doorstep, for coaching him to his side, and for allowing him to still be alive. William asked that all this would not be in vain—that God would protect the baby once more, preserve his life, and give him the opportunity to fulfill the purpose he was born to. And, William asked God to spare him one more loss.

God was merciful; He did just that. Each day, Baby Doe grew stronger. In spite of hypothermia and abandonment for unknown reasons, this newborn had survived.

After one week, the infant was placed in foster care, awaiting adoption into what William believes will be the loving home he deserves. William doesn't know if he'll ever see his little miracle again. However, if the new family is willing, he'd be honored to stay in touch, watch the little boy grow, and continue to be a part of a miracle in progress.

Baby Doe's birth parents have still not been identified. No one knows for certain why this precious angel was abandoned on William's doorstep. But William has an idea. God knew Baby Doe wasn't the only one needing a miracle that cold winter morning. The Lord knew that William needed one, too. This gift of life, joy, and hope has taught William once and for all that, in spite of his dear wife's passing, he still has a purpose. And for that, he will always be grateful.

Out of the Darkness

Through harsh, life-changing experiences, Sarah Carleson has come to understand that illness can strike suddenly, raging through one's existence and leaving in its path both painful and disfiguring symptoms. However, she's also found that there's something more valuable than medicine and so-called cures, whether pharmaceutical or natural. Sarah's been fortunate to discover that the angelic face of a young child, one who is your very own, can change the course of your life and bring about a physical reversal from destructive afflictions.

For Sarah, the summer of 1987 was a time of great upheaval as her family set out to find its place in the world, a place where they could finally begin to settle down and establish roots. Her husband's job required a move from Texas to California, and she was compelled to leave behind a job she enjoyed , as well as dear friends and neighbors she'd grown to love. Within a two-year period they moved three times. She looked for work, left jobs, and looked for work again. However, as a young working mother, Sarah refused to acknowledge her struggle and anxiety. Instead, she tried to support the changes in their lives and threw her strength into providing stability for her two toddlers, Preeya and Premila.

As she cared for her daughters, Sarah chose to ignore the ever-increasing dryness in her eyes, pain in her joints, and fits of insomnia that would strike at will. It took a couple of years, when the symptoms grew worse, before she finally realized the need to seek medical attention.

Sarah hoped the doctor would pinpoint what was causing her body to fail. Perhaps he had some sort of magic pill that would put her back into the high-energy mode she was famous for. Instead, after weeks of tests and retests, he came up with a diagnosis that did not carry the option of a cure, magic or otherwise. Sarah was diagnosed with systemic lupus. Her doctor explained that there were different degrees of this disease, and that although time would tell where Sarah's would take her, no matter what the outcome, she was in for a journey upon a rough and hazardous road.

Being an optimist and one not accustomed to being ill, she went into an immediate mode of denial. Sarah was certain that if she just ignored the symptoms, pulled her tired and aching body out of bed, she would forget the pain and life would return to normal. She was wrong. After a few more years of noncompliance, taking medications only as she saw fit and pushing herself to the limit, Sarah ended up in serious trouble.

There were visits to the emergency room in the middle of the night. Her husband would bundle her up and carry her to the car. She'd moan in agony, leaving them both terrified of what was happening and uncertain of how to make it stop. There were hospital admissions where she would lay for days, having steroids pumped into her veins to bring her immune system back to a survivable level. Eventually, Sarah caught on. She had no choice but to come to terms with her disease, accept that it was real, and adjust her life to accommodate its presence.

There came an end to overdoing, something all women with families consider part of their everyday existence. There came naps in the afternoon and having to let go of being the perfect wife, mother, relative, friend, and neighbor. Sarah had come to understand that she couldn't do it all and continue to survive.

As the years went on and the quality of her life worsened, she began to experience depression. Sarah began to think she was not benefiting her husband, children, or anyone else. She was in pain every day, all the time, and had absolutely no energy even to make her way down the hall to retrieve a simple glass of water. Sarah felt helpless and useless and saw no light at the end of this dark and long tunnel.

Added to this was the discouragement she felt when she looked in the mirror and saw the effect the steroids had on her swollen face and body. She did not recognize the woman she was becoming. "Surely," she felt, "this cannot be me." But it was. Not usually driven by vanity, Sarah was still discouraged by the sabotage the medication that gave her life was now doing to her appearance. Call it what you will, but her changing physical image gave to her depression an intensity that she had not expected.

Eventually, Sarah began to give up and look for a way out. She decided that if her doctor could not provide the cure or at least give her hope of mild improvement, then there was no point in living. If she could not control this affliction, she was determined to at least control its outcome. She gave up trying to recover, gave up believing, and, finally, gave up her very desire to exist. Sarah wanted to put an end to her suffering and what she perceived was the anguish inflicted upon her family.

In 1992, as her hopelessness became unshakable, Sarah desperately reached out to the Lord in prayer. "Please, God, show me a way out. Help me to understand my circumstances and to find a way out of the darkness." Soon afterward, Sarah attended a lupus support group and encountered Carol, a slender, dark-haired woman who had survived the disease for more than a decade. This was exactly what Sarah had been waiting for. In all her years of treatment, Sarah had never read about or met anyone who seemed to come through to the other side, someone to give her the faith she needed to believe. Carol may not have been the floodlight Sarah was looking for, but she did carry a small flickering candle, one that Sarah could see slightly illuminated at the end of the tunnel. Carol gave Sarah her first glimmer of hope.

Within a few days, Premila and Preeya, now six and seven, began having nightmares. They would awaken in the middle of the night, crying and unable to go back to sleep. Their dreams consisted of various versions of Sarah dying and leaving them motherless. Although she never discussed just how desperate she'd become, their instincts seemed to sense that death was imminent. Her daughters taught Sarah something that would later save her life: her children clearly needed her. They made Sarah understand that her thinking had been warped. She realized that her children simply needed their mother, not a woman in perfect health. With that, she began to get well.

Sarah's recovery was not overnight. Nor was it as some would classify miraculous. She still takes low dosages of medication, continues to know her limits, and respects her need for rest. For the most part, however, she remains happily symptom-free.

If it were not for an answer to a prayer—the glimmer of a dimly lit candle held by a stranger in a support group and then the illuminated torch lit by her two young daughters—Sarah would not have found her way out of that tunnel. The girls are Sarah's angels, the angels that lit her way, guiding her out of the darkness.

Angels in Lace

Adorned with soft curls, an angel in lace dances before her. She places a tender kiss upon her cheek that unmistakably says, "I love you." Barb Livingston yearned for that vision as she awaited the birth of her third child. She and her husband had already been blessed with two beautiful sons. They loved them immensely. They were God's gifts, and Barb knew it. Their lives were filled with happy sights and sounds, bumps and crashes, big hugs, and an occasional pet worm or two. Barb was certain that this time, with her third pregnancy, God would not mind if she attempted to influence Him just a bit. Her intention, of course, was never to dictate, but merely to guide Him in the right direction. After all, in case He hadn't noticed, a change of pace was somewhat overdue in their home. She had well-thought-out plans to exchange denim overalls for delicate dresses, wagons for baby dolls, and crew cuts for pigtails.

However, God, it seemed, had different plans. One afternoon, while reading Psalms 139, Barb saw that He alone made such decisions:

> *I will praise thee; for I am fearfully and wonderfully made: marvelous are thy works; and that my soul knoweth right well.*
>
> *My substance was not hid from thee, when I was made in secret, and curiously wrought in the lowest parts of the earth.*
>
> *Thine eyes did see my substance, yet being imperfect; and in thy book all my members were written, which in continuance were fashioned, when as yet there was none of them.*

Now, Barbara understood. God knew us before we were born, while still in the womb, creating each delicate, inward part. Surely, He could not be second-guessed. As Barb read, she stood humbled at this age-old wisdom. She cannot say how, but at that point Barb did not simply resign herself to God's plan. Instead, she gave herself over to it. Clearly, He knew just who her third child would be, had known since the beginning of time, and now this was the only baby she desired. Boy or girl, Barb knew this child would be exactly who she was meant to nurture, cherish, and share her life with.

Soon their newborn arrived, and they named him Jonathan, "God's gracious gift." He was a beautiful boy, a dearly loved son, and one who has lived up to his name in every way. He added to their family and home more love, more hugs, and yes, even a few more worms. As life progressed, Barb's children grew, and their family dynamics began to change.

Many years passed, and as we often do, Barb forgot her dream, but God did not. In time, Jonathan and his young wife, Kristi, delivered two beautiful babies of their own. In His grace, the Lord remembered the desire that grew in Barb's heart many seasons before, a seed that He'd gently watered over the years, one He had, in fact, planted Himself. Barb is certain God answers prayer, that He hears the secret whispers of our hearts. She's sure of this every time she sees her granddaughters, Madison and Marissa, adorned with soft curls, like angels in lace dancing before her. Most of all, she knows it's true when they place tender kisses upon her cheek that unmistakably say, "I love you."

The Dress

War is a tragic and difficult reality of life. In its brutal path, it manages to leave behind much heartache and human suffering. Sometimes, it is the horrible, even unspeakable, events that we remember. However, on occasion, it is the basic, nagging ache in a soldier's heart, an ache that cannot be relieved except by seeing once again the images that are familiar, the faces of family and close friends.

Many years ago, during World War II, when Joe Butto was only 20, he had the opportunity to experience something that has stayed clear in his memory for more than five decades. This remembrance has taught him that when loneliness is at its peak and discouragement and fear strike at his very soul, each silent cry is heard by a faithful God who understands.

While stationed in China and resting on a simple cot alongside his buddies, Joe prepared to go to sleep. Certainly, this environment was nothing like the greatly missed comforts of his own soft and warm bed covered with quilts, in his modest but wonderful home in Roseville, California. Joe, like all his fellow soldiers, missed his family, his friends, and the warmth and security of the simple life back in America. He wanted nothing more than to return immediately, but knew there was a greater mission to accomplish for freedom. Joe realized that as much as he wanted his personal dreams fulfilled, they would simply have to wait for an undisclosed duration of time.

While he rested, he's not sure, even to this day, what led him to glance in the direction of a large crate beside his cot, but he did. As Joe looked, he saw something that continues to baffle him, even 50 years after the fact. There, as clear as she could be, sat a close friend from back in the states. She was wearing a navy blue dress decorated with the print of delicate white flowers. Her long blonde hair gently cascaded over her shoulders. She said nothing, and Joe must admit, he didn't dare speak himself. She simply smiled at him reassuringly, as one friend comforts another. Joe bolted upright in bed, rubbed his eyes, moved the mosquito netting over his cot, and watched her for about five minutes. Eventually, no longer alarmed by her presence, he closed his eyes to rest. Moments later, when he reopened them, she was no longer there.

The next morning, Joe dismissed the fear of being disbelieved and told his bunkmates everything that happened the night before. He assured them that he had not been dreaming or hallucinating, and to his surprise, no one uttered a single laugh or voiced even the slightest doubt or criticism. These were men at war, men who didn't know what today, let alone tomorrow, would bring, and who didn't take lightly any encouragement from home, heaven-sent or otherwise.

It makes Joe smile, to this very day, when he remembers the singular response of his wartime buddies. That night, every one of them, without an exception, moved a crate closer to their bedside, as if silently inviting a friendly guest from home to join them for a much welcomed visit.

About a year later, with the war over, Joe excitedly returned to the United States. The joy of seeing his country, family, friends, and small town overwhelmed him. When he had the opportunity to see Dorothy, the young woman in his vision, he surprised himself by telling her what he'd seen that night in China. She asked Joe to describe the dress she was wearing. When he did, she calmly got up, walked to her closet, and pulled out the exact navy blue outfit, he had seen in his vision. The dress? It had been purchased after Joe left for China.

Why did Dorothy appear to Joe that night? Was she, as some would say, merely the hallucination of a lonely and frightened young soldier? Or was she what Joe believes, a vision or an angel representing friendship, assuring him that his sorrow was understood? Joe will always remember that God chose to send exactly what he needed. He sent a visitor in the form of an old friend to comfort him.

The Single Mom and the Home on the Golf Course

*A*ll parents who truly comprehend the gift God has given them dream the absolute best for their children: health, love, the happiest childhood possible, and the potential to grow and become the very best they were created to be.

Esther Gomez was no exception. She loved her four, dark-haired children—Veronica, Sylvia, Laura, and Danny—more than she is able to express. But Esther was up against the odds; she was a young mother recently abandoned by her husband in California. However, even such a harsh and unfair reality could not stop her from believing. And Esther didn't just believe for herself; her truest dreams involved her dear children, whom she believed deserved so much better. In spite of what seemed like overwhelming obstacles, Esther's faith rested in God, knowing that He not only understood but also dreamt with her.

It was the autumn of 1975, and Esther observed her children, ranging in ages from 8 to 13, growing up in a neighborhood that was disintegrating before her very eyes. Maybe it had always been that way, or maybe it suddenly appeared more clearly because God was preparing a miracle.

Esther prayed daily for a safe, happy neighborhood in which she could raise her young family. She desired a place where friendships could be made that would last a lifetime, a place where schools were clean and where teachers hadn't given up hope.

On one afternoon, soon after her prayers began, Esther took her faith a step further. She drove around town, randomly searching for a house, not knowing exactly what she was looking for, but certain that when she saw it, she would somehow know.

On this very day, on her first time out to look, Esther did find "The House." As she drove past perfectly manicured lawns and a lovely, green, inviting golf course, Esther saw a "For Sale" sign, and she knew. To this day, she has trouble describing how she was certain that this was "home," except to say that when she saw it, something leaped inside her, and as clearly as she knew God was able, she knew this was the one—this was her answer to prayer.

Esther drove home in anticipation. She called a realtor friend and told him of the house, the one she was so positive was intended for her family. The friend was also a man of faith, but ever practical, he did not believe in so-called "real estate miracles." He told Esther to forget it. The listing showed it was available for $75,000 (the equivalent of three times that amount today). He explained it would sell quickly, since it was a fair price in a desirable neighborhood. But Esther insisted. "This is my children's home," she said. "I just know it; you have to take me there!"

Not wanting to disappoint his friend, he reluctantly drove Esther to the house. The owner was not at home, but the realtor had a key. While he waited in the hall, Esther wandered excitedly through the house. As she walked into each and every room, Esther's faith grew within her. It was everything she had prayed for, and the money, well that was something she knew the Lord could provide. As Esther entered each bedroom, she imagined her children sleeping safely in their warm and cozy beds. When she entered the big, spacious kitchen with windows overlooking the perfectly groomed golf course, Esther saw her family at the table, laughing and talking while she prepared homemade tortillas. In the spacious family room, Esther envisioned her children playing with their friends on a rainy afternoon or sitting around the television on a quiet evening, accompanied by a roaring fire in the huge rock fireplace that sat invitingly in the corner. Yes, there was no doubt, this was it!

In the middle of Esther's vision, she was jolted back to reality when the owner of the house walked in the front door.

"Make an offer!" she excitedly told her agent.

Her realtor looked slightly embarrassed, not wanting to propose a ridiculous amount. But, if merely out of obligation and in hope that the rejection might somehow bring Esther back to reality, he asked the owner to call his representative. When the listing agent arrived, they wrote out an offer for $45,000. The owner responded to Esther's heartfelt hope with spontaneous laughter. He stayed firm to his $75,000 price tag and told her to stop wasting his time.

With only the faith of a woman who's certain God has spoken, she looked this man in the eye and gently said, "This house is meant for my children. It won't sell to anyone else." Then she smiled at the perplexed gentleman and quietly left.

A few months passed, and Esther learned that the owner was soon relocating to another part of the state. Against her agent's advice, Esther listed her home for sale. He tried to explain that even if her home sold and this man accepted her offer, she still could not afford the payments. "It's impossible, Esther," he would tell her over and over again.

"Maybe it's impossible for you and me, but it's not impossible for God," she would reply in faith.

Some days, Esther would drive by this house, park in the driveway while the man was away at work, and just stare at the home, smiling in assurance and praying for God to intervene. Some nights, when her children were asleep, she'd walk the halls of their rundown home and pray, pleading with God to provide a miracle—not for herself, but for her children, who deserved better.

Esther's home sold quickly, and soon after, on one of her drives past the dream house, she noticed that the "For Sale" sign was missing. For the first time in this entire scenario, Esther experienced real fear. Rushing home, she called her agent and told him what happened. He calmly explained that the home had probably sold, as he knew it would, and advised her to be prepared for the worst. However, when he looked into the status of the house, he was shocked to find that it had not sold at all; the listing had expired.

Flung quickly back into her faith mode, Esther excitedly said, "He has to leave in a few weeks; offer $50,000." The agent did, and the owner accepted. The confused man thought Esther had put some sort of curse on his house. She assured him it was not a spell, but the blessing of God, and His desire to provide a dream for her family.

Other miracles quickly followed. Because Esther could not qualify for a direct mortgage, she assumed the owner's original loan. Her agent was terrified to have her take on such debt and tried to convince her she would surely lose the house in a few short months. You see, Esther's monthly take-home pay was $350, and the house payment was $325. How could she possibly feed, clothe, and provide for her four children with a mere $25.00 a month?

Esther went to her boss, a kind and dedicated doctor, and told him of this home—the one she had dreamed about and the one she was about to own. He knew Esther was a fine, dedicated secretary, one who always worked hard for her money. This kind doctor was touched by the struggling mother of four and wanted to help make Esther's dream come true. He immediately doubled her salary, thus providing the final fulfillment of God's miracle.

Esther and her children lived in that wonderful home for many years. Through God's provision and a dosage of faith, they spent their growing years in an environment that was not only filled with safety and beauty, but with ample love. They did make lifetime friends with the neighborhood children, and their memories are filled with goodness and joy. All of the children still refer to it as their one and only true home.

Through this experience, Esther and her children have come to understand that while we won't always receive everything we ask of the Lord, His plans for us are always good. They will never forget and will forever be grateful that at this time, on this occasion, God, in His grace, heard the heartfelt and unselfish prayer of a young mother and answered joyfully with ready and open arms.

There Really Is a Free Lunch

*B*arbara Johnson is a strong woman of faith. This is not to say her life runs like clockwork and all her prayers are answered just as she would like them to be. Barbara struggles with the best of them and, more often than not, finds herself in a well-occupied waiting room of God's praying people.

Barbara's faith gives her hope: God cares enough to make a difference for all those He loves. It brings joy to her heart to think of His faithfulness at meeting His children's needs, no matter how small they may be. Barbara knows, without a doubt, that where He once has worked, He can work again.

One particular blessing occurred in the mid 1980s, when Barbara's daughter, Pam, was about 10 years old. Barbara's husband, Curtis, had just been laid off from his job. The family experienced a temporary financial setback. For a while, even groceries were hard to come by. One evening, while Pam packed her lunch for school, she found the fridge empty. She looked up at her mom with a sorrowful expression and asked what to do. What would she pack? What would she eat for lunch? Barbara didn't have an answer, but she knew the One who did. Quietly, with the gentleness only a mother of faith can offer, she told her daughter, "The Lord will provide." Pam rolled her eyes at the solution, wanting to receive what she believed to be a more concrete answer, perhaps, a few slices of bologna and a couple pieces of bread. But Barbara's faith remained firm: "The Lord will provide."

The next morning, Pam was not surprised to discover that food had not magically appeared in the cupboards, nor had money appeared in an unmarked envelope upon the doorstep. Barbara was faced with the difficult task of sending Pam off to school without lunch. As she sent her on her way, she remained confident that God would take care of the problem and that somehow Pam, her precious daughter, would not go without.

Immediately after Pam left for school, Barbara fell to her knees, not just asking God to supply a child's much needed meal, but even more important, to supply just the right answer to build a young girl's faith. Barbara spent the morning pleading with God to reassure Pam of His love.

When school was over, she met her daughter with an equal amount of fear and anticipation. But when she saw the young girl, Barbara knew God had been faithful. She found Pam skipping and smiling from ear to ear. "You'll never guess what happened today, Mom. I arrived at school, and my friend was waving two bags in his hands. He told me when he packed his lunch last night, he decided to make extra sandwiches and give one away. And he chose me, Mom, he chose me! The Lord really did provide!"

Shortly after this day, their lives began to change for the better. Curtis was blessed with a new job, and food was no longer scarce in their home. But, during this time of lack, the Johnson family learned a life-changing lesson they will never forget. God blesses his children by providing not only food to fill their stomachs, but faith-building encouragement to fill their souls.

Blossoms from Heaven

Now and then, we all need a little reassurance, not just the kind that comes from our loved ones, but the kind only God Himself can give. When someone we love dies, our faith is stretched and challenged as we attempt to transcend our beliefs from where they rest in our minds and begin to place them firmly in our souls.

My father-in-law was a kind and gentle man. I only met him once, because he lived far away in the Fiji Islands. He visited the United States in the spring of 1992 when I was pregnant with my second child. My husband, Patrick, our five-year-old daughter, Tiffany, and I enjoyed Dad's visit tremendously, taking him everywhere we could to give him a feel for the country his son had so grown to love.

During his stay, I would watch as Dad would carry Tiffany around the yard on his back, walk her to kindergarten, and make her a special lunch like only a grandparent can. Dad kept himself busy, fearing, I'm afraid, that he somehow needed to earn his stay. He painted woodwork, cleaned, and did endless repairs around the house. One of the things he particularly loved to do was garden. Dad's own yard looked like a tropical paradise, and I think he attempted, as futile as it was, to make mine look the same. One afternoon, I bought flowering geraniums in pink, purple, and white, and he planted each of them carefully with love. Unfortunately, the geraniums took a setback, and two of the three died immediately, leaving only the pale pink specimen to survive.

When the month's visit had come to an end, I watched sadly as Patrick drove him to the airport. I'll never forget the intense and studious look on Dad's face. He stared endlessly out the back window as if to paint a permanent picture of me and our home. I wondered why he looked so serious. After all, I imagined that Dad would return in a couple of years. But he knew better.

Four years later, in the spring of 1996, at the age of 57, my father-in-law died suddenly of a heart attack. Devastated, my husband flew to Fiji for the funeral services and to say his final good-byes. On the day of the burial, I sat at home, and as we humans are prone to do, I began to doubt everything I'd always believed. Was there really a heaven? Do God's people live again once this body has withered and died? What I always knew in my head was now being tested and challenged by my heart. I prayed a simple prayer, asking God to reassure me that Dad was really in a better place, that he lived again with God, and that we would someday see him again. It was a sincere cry from the heart, and God was listening.

Jolted from my prayer by a glimpse at the clock, I quickly stepped outside to begin the short walk that would bring Tiffany home from school. Glancing casually into my yard, I noticed something for the very first time. The flowers Dad had planted, the same ones that had died four years earlier, were now alive and in full magnificent bloom. The pale pink survivor was accompanied by the purple and white blossoms as they proudly stood tall, reaching toward the light. I could hardly believe my eyes. As I approached them, I noticed that the new blooms had not rooted at all, but all three now grew from one living shrub. I knew without a doubt that God, in His mercy, had seen fit to reassure me of Dad's flight into heaven by using the very flowers he himself had once planted.

I understand now, more than ever, that although everyone must die and return to the earth, God is able to restore us back to life, in full and magnificent beauty, as we each stand tall, reaching toward the light.

The Nun, the Dream, and the Medical Record

Sometimes we avoid a crisis, put it off, and ultimately postpone it for another day—a day when we're stronger and better able to cope. In 1973, at the age of 21, my sister, Spring, died of cancer. The death of a young person is always difficult to accept, and even harder if it's someone you love. Spring was my only sister—my only sibling—and while she was ill, avoiding the impending loss became my obsession.

Unfortunately, as unresolved grief will do, it followed me all my life, waiting patiently like an unwelcome guest that refused to go home. The postponed sorrow manifested itself in many ways. One of its disguises was in the form of a persistent dream that began after her death and continued for almost 17 years. The plot of the dream rarely varied. I'd receive a call from a nurse who would inform me that Spring, though sick, was still alive. When I'd insist that she'd died some time ago, the caller would assure me a mistake had occurred, that she did in fact remain alive. I would awake to the realization that her death, and not the dream, was all too real.

Years passed, and in the summer of 1989, I took a job at the same hospital in which my sister had died. I tried several ways to locate Spring's medical records. All my attempts proved futile, and I assumed that such extremely old documents had long been destroyed.

A few years later, I had a very different sort of dream. In it, I found myself sitting quietly, looking over Spring's medical file. The dream was so real, so incredibly vivid, that when I awoke, I knew the records did exist and that reading them would somehow bring closure. I quickly called the hospital and explained my story. I was disappointed to hear that, although they felt for my plight, the records were confidential and I would be unable to view them. I was devastated.

I went to work that evening, not only disappointed but, quite frankly, a little angry. Had God been playing some kind of sick joke with my emotions? That night, as I shared my story with my coworkers, one of them suggested I speak to Sister Mary, an administrative nun, who apparently had a great deal of leeway and might be able to "bend the rules." Certainly, she would see the side of healing and compassion as more important than a regulation that was designed arbitrarily.

As we rode in the elevator, my friends convinced me to call in the morning, make an appointment with Sister Mary, and plead my case. Encouraged by this new possibility, I began to have hope. Suddenly, as my friends and I chatted, the elevator doors opened to reveal a nun, adorned in a beautiful, white garment, standing at its entrance. My coworkers gasped as if they'd seen an angel and literally pushed me toward her, chanting, "There she is. Ask her now!"

This "chance" meeting was truly quite remarkable. During my two years at the hospital, I'd never seen Sister Mary on the premises during my evening shift. Nor have I seen her in the many years since. Surely, this was God's providence. Sister Mary had been resting at home when she remembered important papers left carelessly on her desk. She was on her way to retrieve them when we met.

As I shared my story with her, I began to weep. I apologized for being so emotional over events that had occurred many years before. But she was compassionate, understood, and promised to help.

Thanks to Sister Mary, a couple of days later I was given copies of Spring's complete medical records, beginning with her initial symptoms, diagnosis, treatments, and, finally, her death. I read that file, page by page, crying and absorbing all that I could. The last paragraph, documenting her passing, was written so coldly, I realized that the value of human life seems only to register with those who love them and with Him who loves us all.

I know now that everything happened in God's perfect time. He waited patiently for me to let go—and to obtain a specific job—to give me a special dream, to bring Sister Mary to the elevator door at the moment she should not have been there, and, finally, to bring me to a place of true acceptance and healing.

How do I know I've truly been healed? After I finally read the document, 17 years after my sister's death, my recurring dream of death's denial came to an abrupt end. It's been many years since this blessing, and the dream has never dared to manifest itself again. God's timing is both patient and perfect, and His healing complete and whole.

And now, just as I believe that my sister, Spring, rests quietly in heaven, so my soul has also found peace.

The Answer

It was the late 1970s, and Dianne Jackson had just graduated from nursing school. She was excited about her new vocation and began her first job working in the critical care unit of Los Angeles County Hospital. She was optimistic. Dianne knew she couldn't change the world, but she was determined to better the lives of those she came into contact with. She wanted to show compassion to each patient placed under her care and also to their family members, who struggled with fears and concerns for their loved ones.

However, she never anticipated the challenge her first patient would present. Nursing school didn't prepare Dianne for patients like Sharon* or for family members like her husband, Jim.* Sharon was a beautiful woman, in her mid-twenties, admitted for end-stage lupus. Limited by her body's ability to continue fighting the disease and by the medical science of her time, she could no longer hang on. Sharon was dying.

Dianne knew death was as much a part of the nursing profession as healing. However, she didn't expect to be confronted so early in her career by the tragic loss of one so young. So close in age to her patient, the young nurse began to reflect on her own mortality. It was a struggle to deal with the questions present in her own heart: the whys, the searching for a purpose, a reason, a justification. It was even more difficult to deal with Jim's questions and his anger, confusion, and bitterness—the torment from a young man about to lose his heart and soul, his beloved wife.

Sharon was a woman of strong faith. She had recently stopped praying for her own healing, accepting that the outcome had finally been determined, understanding that God had a pur-

---

*Names followed by an asterisk are pseudonyms.

pose, even if she did not yet know what it was. But Jim was different. He was angry, furious at a God who would dare to snatch the love of his life away from him. He raged at God, cursing Him for his wife's condition, and poured out an angry and bitter heart to Dianne.

Soon it became apparent that Jim, in fact, needed healing as well. Dianne began to worry that after Sharon's death, Jim would never recover, that he'd go off into the world unable to fully cope. Her concern shifted from caring for the primary patient to caring for a man whose problems she was not equipped to handle. Sharon also began to pray, not for herself, but for her husband, Jim.

At the same time, it was announced that Kathryn Kuhlman would be having a crusade in the area. This flamboyant evangelist was famous for her strong faith in the healing power of God. When Jim heard the announcement on the radio, he responded with a flicker of hope. It was expected that people from all around would bring their loved ones: the sick, the desperate, and the dying. They would come with canes, in wheelchairs, or in some cases, be carried, but they were all seeking the same thing—a miracle. And so was Jim. Although he'd clearly lost his faith, he was willing to try anything if there was even the smallest chance his wife would be healed. That night, without coaxing from anyone, Jim attended in proxy for Sharon.

During the crusade, Dianne stayed at Sharon's bedside. As the evening wore on, Sharon's vital signs dropped to a critical level. It was clear that she had only moments left on earth. Dianne was desperate to make Jim understand that she had done her best, that God understood his broken heart, but that for reasons we'll never fully understand, it was his wife's time to go. And she was desperate to find Jim.

Not knowing how else to alert him, Dianne called the Los Angeles County Sheriff's Department. She explained that her patient's husband was in attendance at the Kathryn Kuhlman crusade, that his wife had only moments to live, and that she knew he would want to be there. The officers immediately went into action.

Somehow, they located Jim in the crusade and escorted him back to the hospital.

When he arrived, Dianne was afraid to look up. She couldn't bear to see Jim's anger, his hurt, or the fury at a God he had forgotten still loved him. But when their eyes met, she knew a miracle had occurred at the crusade after all. For as she looked directly at Jim, she saw the countenance of a man no longer in torment, a man filled with peace, acceptance, and serenity. It was clear that Jim had been in the very presence of God. He had seen miracles at the crusade, healings all around him. But Jim had also observed those who were not healed, and for the first time, he began to accept God's sovereignty. Although the Lord does not always answer our prayers the way we want Him to, Jim finally understood that God is good, that He looks upon all the sorrows of humanity with great compassion.

Only moments after he arrived at her bedside, Jim said his good-byes. He told Sharon he loved her, that he would never forget her, and that he was grateful for the time God had given them together. And then she was gone.

Dianne realized in that moment that God hears even the weakest cries from the heart—that miracles really do happen. Although Jim's prayers for his wife's healing were not answered as he desired, Sharon's prayers for her husband were. The night Jim lost his beloved wife was the very night he found his soul.

The Dream

Anastasia Lovett never doubted there was a purpose for her life, that she was wanted and loved, that her very existence was nothing short of a miracle. By all reasons of logic, she should never have been born. Her birth was a testament to the grace of God and His perfect plan for her life.

Before Anastasia was born, her parents, Stella and George, already had one child, a lovely daughter who was much loved and the center of their universe. They wanted more children, having so much to give, but circumstances appeared to rule otherwise. Stella had surgery that made her doctor quite certain that any future pregnancies were an impossibility. And for ten years, they were certain he was right.

That is, until the day Stella determined she was pregnant. Excited with the prospect of another child, a miracle baby, she told George. Her husband responded with mixed emotions of hope and doubt. "How could this be happening?" he wondered. "Hadn't the experts said that such a blessed event could never be?" But, leaning on Stella's confidence, they went to see her doctor.

When they arrived for their appointment, they were quickly ushered into a private room. Immediately after the doctor entered, the story came pouring out. Stella was having a baby! The stern physician tried to hide his disbelief and then shook his head repeatedly. "No," he told her. "You cannot be pregnant." The mere words of a trained medical professional were not enough to deter Stella. She begged the doctor to perform tests, but he flatly refused. "There's no reason to run any tests, Stella. A pregnancy for you is a medical impossibility."

After a brief examination, the doctor added more bad news—a second surgery was necessary to clean the uterus, and it should be done as soon as possible. But Stella firmly refused the medical treatment, understanding it meant the end to her pregnancy, certain death to the young baby growing inside her, and an end, in fact, to her miracle. The doctor took George aside and offered a warning. "Your wife is not dealing with reality. For her own health, you must convince her to have this procedure immediately."

Sad and confused, the couple quietly left the office. As the days progressed, George begged his wife to go back to the doctor for further treatment. But she flatly refused. Stella was protecting her baby in the only way she knew. She would not change her mind, no matter what.

One evening, before bedtime, when the pressure from her husband and doctor grew unbearable, she began to pray. Stella asked God for a sign to help her make such a crucial decision. "Dear Lord, should I follow the doctor's advice and seek medical treatment, or am I really pregnant? You must tell me. You're the only One I can truly trust." That night, Stella had a dream, a dream so real, so vivid, that it seemed more like a vision than anything else. In her dream she saw a young girl, about ten years of age, sitting on a swing, dark hair flowing, short bangs, and a smile that would not leave her presence. And when Stella woke up, she knew.

After the dream, there wasn't an expert in the world who could convince Stella she wasn't expecting. She simply told everyone who looked on with doubt, "You'll see what God has done. If you wait, you'll believe in miracles, too." And soon they did. Before long, it became apparent that Stella was pregnant, and the reluctant doctor was forced to perform tests that confirmed it to be true. He had no explanation, but Stella had one. It was God, nothing more, nothing less; of this, she never doubted.

When the time came, Anastasia was born, an uneventful delivery but with miraculous beginnings. With no surprise to Stella, her young daughter grew to look exactly like the little girl in her dream, the very dream that had spared her baby's life.

Anastasia is a mature woman now, with three grown children and a grandchild of her own. She believes that all babies are gifts from God, orchestrated by perfect plan and design. Of course she believes in miracles. After all, Anastasia is a miracle herself.

The Gift

In the mid 1980s, leaving the shelter of her warm and nurturing Northern California home, Kim Tricomo set out to find her place in the world. She missed her mother's wonderful meals—baked chicken on a cold winter evening, served with fresh biscuits and honey, and a steaming bowl of minestrone soup. She was homesick for the familiar touch of the cool, flower-print sheets in her childhood bed and for the sweet-smelling, yellow roses blooming abundantly in their large front yard. But most of all, she missed the late-night conversations with her mother, tender heartfelt moments that she longed to experience again.

Kim hadn't traveled far from her family's home, just a few, short hours away, yet things were quite different now. A new world awaited her, and Kim was struck with the harsh realities of college life. It was different being on her own. There were bills to pay and responsibilities to fulfill. There were days she questioned the purpose and meaning of all she wanted to accomplish. Missing her loved ones and struggling to fit into her new environment, Kim asked God to teach her more about His purpose, to grant her lessons in love, life, and truth.

It was about this time that she took a position as the manager of a local fast food restaurant. Her job was solely intended to supply the necessary funds to continue her education. It was relatively easy work and would not interfere with her studies.

Kim was responsible for offering friendly service to her customers, and she proudly did just that. For the most part, she was able to maintain a positive attitude, but on occasion, there were those who tested her patience to the limits, those who were never satisfied no matter what she did to accommodate them. Some people, it seemed, were "takers." Kim and her staff knew that the customer was "always right," yet their frustration with trying to make everyone happy made their jobs occasionally stressful. That is, until the day Kim met Ben.

Ben was a homeless man who began wandering into her shop with increased frequency. He would often bring to her counter scattered change: a few dimes, nickels, and pennies, no doubt gathered from the donation of kind strangers, to purchase a warm and soothing cup of coffee. He always requested his beverage with a broad smile and received it with a polite "thank you." For many of Kim's coworkers, it seemed, his presence was somewhat of a nuisance. For them, Ben was someone to serve as quickly as possible in hopes that he'd leave before he scared off the "real" customers. But for Kim, Ben was a presence to be reckoned with, a test of grace, kindness, and understanding.

Of course, she often wondered how his life had reached this point—wandering the cold streets, existing on handouts and an occasional free meal. She wondered if he had made poor life choices or had simply succumbed to mental illness. Whatever the reason, Kim didn't allow the cause of Ben's predicament to color her view of him, to affect the way she chose to respond to him as a human being. Perhaps some people might argue that Kim was nothing more than an enabler, someone who should have encouraged Ben to "pull himself up by his bootstraps" and make something of his life. But she felt they had met for another reason, for a different sort of purpose, a purpose not intended for judgment but simply to show Ben the kindness and dignity that all human beings deserve.

And so one afternoon, Kim purchased lunch for Ben. At first, he was reluctant to take a meal from her, seeming to test Kim's very determination to give. But she won, and Ben, for the first time in days, had a hot meal.

Kim asked him to return daily, and so he did. Weeks went by, and Ben ate with a polite "thank you" and a smile. One rainy afternoon, after Ben finished his meal, he quietly approached Kim. Ben reached into his tattered backpack and offered her a priceless treasure—the only thing he had to give—a smooth, oval rock that he'd been saving for just such an occasion. Kim promised Ben she would keep it forever and that whenever she gazed upon it, she would remember him with fondness. And so she did.

After that day, Kim never saw Ben again. She soon graduated from college, left her fast food job, and went on to become a fine teacher of elementary school children. But through the years, she's kept her promise. That rock has followed her from place to place and finally to the home she now shares with her husband and two young sons. For most, whose eyes never met Ben's, the "gift" appears as nothing more than a cold and drab rock. But when she gazes at that gray, smooth stone, she sees something that most do not. Kim sees an answer to prayer, a lesson in giving, a lesson in love, a lesson she will never forget.

The Visitor

*L*orre Long didn't quite know how it happened. She'd always dreamed of being married and raising children. Now, that precious dream was crumbling around her. She was a wife and the mother of a young toddler, Brandon. She thought life was perfect. That is, until 1992, when her husband announced he wanted a divorce. Out of the blue, just like that. All her dreams, all her securities, came tumbling down around her.

Shattered, Lorre took Brandon, packed their bags, left California, and headed for home. For Lorre, home was a small town in Iowa, filled with gentle people, childhood friends, happy memories, and most of all, the rest and compassion that only her family could provide. In that place of refuge, she and her son were embraced by loved ones who brought comfort to their weary souls and helped them see there was hope for the future, a reason to believe they could go on.

One Sunday morning, while attending church, she felt particularly dejected. Where was God? Was He real? Did He know the disappointment in her heart? And if so, did He really care? She listened to the music, trying her best to sing along. Her heart wanted nothing more than to cry out for help, for any sign, that the lyrics were true.

When the priest rose to speak, she noticed he was new. In town for only a week, this visitor, Father Gielow, was to offer the morning sermon. As the quiet and gentle man spoke of God's heart, of His concern for our needs, it was as if he spoke to Lorre alone. He shared that while many times we suffer, God is readily available with comfort and a good plan for our lives. Father Gielow looked directly into Lorre's eyes, piercing through her soul, as if he knew more than he could, as if God had shared her heart with his.

A few days later, while she was outside mowing her lawn, Father Gielow drove past her house. He recognized her, stopped, and asked if they could talk. Lorre quickly obliged. They sat down on the porch and began to chat. Father Gielow told her that on Sunday, when he looked in her eyes, he could see pain. He offered a prayer and a message of hope and faith: "God loves you. Everything will be all right." When he left, Lorre knew things would be different. Oh, she didn't expect them to change overnight, but she knew that no matter what, God was watching over her and her young son. She knew He saw their broken hearts and would lead them upon a new and better path.

And so He did. From that day forward, their lives began to grow and change for the better. Their faith had been restored, their souls touched. They watched as, day by day, God continued to meet their needs. The months with Lorre's family had been healing, had brought strength and comfort.

In time, soon after Father Gielow's kind words of encouragement, Lorre met a wonderful man, Darrin, fell in love, and with everyone's blessings, married. And, now, with the addition of a new baby boy, Nicholas, they are a happy family of four. Lorre knows she has received the fulfillment of a promise, a heaven-sent message to a young woman in need, a woman whose life has been changed forever by love.

On Eagles' Wings

D utch Deiling was a devoted husband and father. He was much loved by his wife, Neva, and their three beautiful daughters. Dutch shared with his family the values he so strongly held, the strength that's gained from faith, and the powerful belief that God loves everyone.

The Deiling family attended church together in their small Iowa town each and every Sunday morning. It was more than a tradition; it was the very source from which they drew their strength. Dutch especially loved the worship music. He found it encouraging and uplifting. But no song affected him the way "On Eagles' Wings" did. Whenever he heard it, he would smile at his family and sing with enthusiasm. To Dutch, the song spoke of God's grace and willingness to carry us through our problems as if on the very wings of eagles. When the music played, he would feel his burdens lift, as if they'd somehow left his presence and begun to take flight.

In 1990, everything changed. Dutch discovered he had cancer. Devastated, he quietly told his family, the very people he loved more than life itself. But Dutch was determined to be strong for his wife and grown children. He would live, by example, the very faith he had always taught them to trust in. His family wasn't so sure. How would they survive without his presence, his love, the very strength he had always offered? Through the crisis of their impending loss, they began to wonder if God really loved them. Dutch prayed that God would comfort his family.

On the day he was buried, many came to say their final good-byes: relatives, friends, neighbors, and of course his wife, daughters, and grandchildren. It was clear from the gathering of mourners that Dutch was a man much loved, one who would truly be missed.

His family chose the music to play at the memorial: "On Eagles' Wings." For the first time, they began to realize what the song had meant to him all those years. They sang with their hearts—for God, for themselves, and for Dutch.

Since his passing, the Deiling family continues to feel the comforting presence of God. Whenever they have a special event—a graduation, the baptism of a new child, any sacred moment they wish Dutch could share—they hear the song and think of Dutch. Often the song is played without their special request. But these beautiful and touching lyrics have taken on new meaning to their family. It speaks to them of comfort, love, strength, and the faithfulness of a God who will never leave them, a God who hears their cries and mends their broken hearts. Most of all, when the soft music plays, they feel heaven gently remind them not to fear, that Dutch has been lifted up, as if on the wings of eagles, into the very arms of God.

The Letter

ecisions. They can be stumbling blocks, leaving us afraid to retreat, afraid to move forward, simply paralyzed in time. During the 1970s, Sue Renz had dropped out of college, but in 1986, she contemplated going back to finish her degree. She had always wanted to help people, and a degree in psychology seemed to draw her in that direction. However, the mere possibility of starting over gave Sue a headache—signing up, finding transportation, balancing conflicting family schedules, writing term papers, and struggling with mountains of tuition. Yet as much as she wanted to dismiss the notion, it returned over and over, forcing her to consider it, to reevaluate the possibility that she was not a quitter.

During this time, Sue had been scheduled to attend a Woman's Christian Retreat. While there, she planned to seek God and ask Him what to do. The retreat was wonderful. Sue enjoyed the teaching and appreciated the time of solitude. On a crisp afternoon, she sat down on a bench, breathed in the fresh, pine-scented air, and began to pray. "God, I wish you could just write a letter, put it down on paper, and send it to me. Then I'd know what to do." No sooner had she uttered those words when a woman approached her. "I have something for you. I wrote it this morning, and during prayer, I felt inspired to give it to you." Sue took the note, and as the woman walked away, began to read:

> *His grace is sufficient for the hour. He is calling forth your name. You have said in your heart, "I am not worthy." God has need of you to serve others. Come to Him, let Him release your burdens. Put on his Yoke for it is easy. . . . He has prepared this time for your release. Be not afraid to walk forward. He will uphold you with His mighty arms.*

What did this mean? Could it be an answer to prayer, a letter from the heart of God? As she began to read it over and over again, Sue was convinced it was a sign.

Sue met with a college counselor and poured out her heart. Her car would never make it to the campus. But there was an answer. The counselor advised Sue that there was an extension course close to her home. But what about her family's busy schedule? How could she possibly take time out for school? Again there was an answer; the program was offered only a few evenings a week. Everything looked perfect. But there was only one hitch. The entire package would cost $6,000. Well, that was it. Sue could no more get her hands on $6,000 than $6,000,000. Satisfied that it was settled, she headed for home.

As she walked in the front door, the telephone rang. It was her father; he had a question. Sue's brother had spoken with him just that morning and was wondering, would she be too proud to accept financial help? He could afford $500 a month—a gift, plain and simple, no strings attached. Sue quickly thanked him and said, "Yes!" How grateful she was for her brother's generosity. It was only later, when she sat down to take it all in, that she realized $500 per month added up to $6,000 a year—the exact amount of her tuition. God had been faithful. And He was good at math!

Sue finished her degree in business psychology. She had finally graduated; she was no longer a quitter. Sue has used that degree to help others with her personal counsel and to pursue a career as a self-employed business woman. The letter proved true; God upheld Sue with His mighty arms. And now, no longer afraid, she continues to walk forward.

A Blessing in Disguise

It was October in Iowa, with crisp orange leaves crackling underfoot, and a young family was rejoicing in the birth of a healthy baby boy. A beautiful picture, except for one real problem: a short bank account at the end of the month and payday an entire week away.

Nineteen ninety-six had been a good year for Lorre Long. She adored her husband, Darrin; five-year-old son, Brandon; and precious baby boy, Nicholas. She was thrilled to be a wife and mother, but her cloud of joy was stifled by unexpected bills, a temporary financial setback, and a sense of pride that kept her from asking anyone for help.

Lorre had always been the type of soul who offered assistance to anyone in need. She did this as part of her firm belief that to give to another was in fact giving to God. She had never thought poorly of others in need, and yet somehow, with the situation reversed, she felt shame in asking for help. Surely, if she had only hinted, many would have gladly come to her aid. Yet, Lorre chose to share her heart with God alone.

While attending church on Sunday morning, she prayed for her struggling family. She didn't know how God would provide, but she knew, with all her faith, that He would. Walking out of the chapel with her family, she greeted friends and fellow worshippers. No one knew that Lorre had a burden in her heart, one she was unable to carry. No, she was not going to tell a soul, not going to allow a sad look on her face to indicate that anything was amiss.

When her family arrived home that afternoon, waiting on their porch to greet them was a large, shaggy, and very hungry dog. Somehow this canine had lost his way, taken refuge from the cold, and landed on, of all places, her front porch. She patted his head and comforted his weary soul. Her young son squealed and giggled with delight, begging his mother to let him keep the dog. But Lorre knew that this fellow had a home of his own; it was just up to her to find out where it was.

She brought out a bowl of water and began to speak in a soothing voice. "Don't worry. Are you hungry?" The last thing she needed at this point in her life was a dog to feed, especially somebody else's dog, but she couldn't ignore the look in his eyes. Lorre did the only thing she knew how to do; she went to her kitchen, found some scraps of leftover food, and fed the poor dog, praying all the while that the owner would soon be found.

The next morning, her husband sat in his chair reading the paper. This was not his customary habit, but that day Lorre was glad that he did. An ad in the "Lost Pets" section caught his eye. Lorre called the number, and the excited owner promised to gather his children and pick up the dog immediately.

In less than 15 minutes, they arrived on her porch, excited pooch jumping, owner smiling, and two young children running from their car, ecstatic with joy. They had found their lost pet, Jake! The grateful gentleman explained that his kids had been heartbroken at the loss of their precious dog. They had prayed that someone kind would find Jake, feed him, and protect him from harm. Their prayers had been answered. And so were Lorre's. The owner reached into his pocket and handed her a reward—a crisp fifty dollar bill. At first she refused, but the owner insisted. As they thanked each other, Lorre smiled. She knew without a doubt that God had provided for her loved ones in a most unusual way. He had answered her prayer with a blessing in disguise, a blessing in the form of a big, shaggy dog. And on that very night, Lorre's thankful family celebrated with a feast.

A Sign in the Heavens

In March of 1979, a simple glance out the window changed Bev Harrelson's life forever. Since that time, she has never for a moment doubted the existence of God. When problems make her wonder where the Lord might be, she needs only to reflect back to that magical night, and she knows the answer.

The miracle began the night of her father's fiftieth birthday. Bev, a lovely young woman of 21, was scurrying about wrapping presents and confirming dinner reservations at her father's favorite Chinese restaurant. Her childhood friend had just arrived at the door to join them for the celebration. The two young women had been close their entire lives. They were raised across the street from one another and shared many special memories—their first bicycles, hugs and tears, silly childhood arguments, and a lifelong, loyal friendship.

During the previous few weeks, Bev had opened up to her friend. Oh, she could have talked to anyone, but Bev knew this confidante was a good listener, and her friend's strong faith in God was just what she needed. The recent breakup of a romantic relationship had left Bev confused, wounded, and struggling. During their quiet talks, Bev had revealed a growing awareness of her need for God. The two had chatted on several occasions, and her friend had been praying for a miracle, a miracle to restore Bev's faith.

While her friend waited patiently beside her, Bev put the finishing touches on her makeup. Bev was beautiful, of delicate, Scandinavian descent, one who looked great with or without adornment. However, although she looked gorgeous on the outside, her heart was broken on the inside. She wanted to believe, wanted to accept her childhood faith. But was it real?

While Bev grabbed shoes from the closet, her friend casually glanced out the window. She was amazed, if not confused, by what she saw. Oh, it was clear what it was, but why was it there, and what in the world did it mean? With a quiver in her voice and afraid to reveal the secret, she asked Bev to look outside. When Bev did, they both stopped cold. There it was, as clear as it could be, a vision, the image of an immense cross, glowing white in the sky, a sign in the heaven, one that neither one of them could deny.

The girls stared at the image for several minutes, discussed what it could mean, left the room, and got Bev's father. When they all came back to the window, it was gone. As mysteriously as the cross had appeared, it had left, quietly, without warning. It was simply there and then gone again. It was only then they understood that the image was a vision meant only for them, an answer to a prayer for Bev's wounded faith.

After that evening, everything changed. That's not to say Bev's life was perfect. There were many hardships awaiting her in the years to follow. But, of this night, she would never forget, could never deny, that God was real and had heard her prayers, the very cries from her heart. He had answered in a miraculous way neither of them could have hoped for or imagined.

How do I know so much about that night? You see, I'm Bev's childhood friend. We shared this miracle together, and because of what we experienced, our lives have never again been the same.

A Perfect Baby

We all have a gift, a desire that is placed in our hearts from birth, something that makes us move in the right direction. For Lisa Grefe, a love for children was her gift. Ever since childhood, she had a compassion for them that never wavered. As a young girl in the 1960s, she would often be found tenderly rocking her baby doll, quietly singing a lullaby. When Lisa was in her twenties, she worked with abused and neglected children, opening her heart and offering comfort to their delicate, wounded souls. Thanks to Lisa, many children didn't give up and knew there was good in the world. Lisa offered proof that not all people were harsh, abusive, and cruel. Many adults, in fact, were gentle and understood the priceless value of a child, knew they were gifts from God, gifts not to abandon but to treasure.

Over the years, Lisa expected to have a family. She had planned to marry and bear many children. Everyone who knew her never doubted this would happen. With Lisa, having children was a given. But sometimes, of course, life takes different turns than we expect, leads us along paths we'd never have taken if given the choice. Lisa's life did just that.

Waiting to find the right man, she didn't meet Bill until her late thirties. Bill was a kind man, strong in stature yet gentle in spirit. Soon, Lisa and Bill fell in love and married. After a few years, with no children on the way, her doctor informed Lisa she must have a hysterectomy. How could this be happening? Why was God cruelly taking away the one dream He Himself had given?

Many prayers were lifted up; many nights went by with no miracle in sight. The surgery was performed on schedule, and God, it seemed, was silent. There was no doubt it was finished; never would Lisa bear children, never would her lifelong desire be fulfilled. Or would it?

About a year later, Lisa and Bill began to look into adoption. Perhaps this was the way God would provide two miracles: a child for Lisa and Bill and a home for a young, innocent baby. Suddenly, the broken dream began to take on a new and hopeful shape. Lisa and Bill began to get excited.

A beautiful baby, Lesly, was delivered to the Grefes, not by the family doctor but by a local social worker. She was an adorable child whose smile looked remarkably like Lisa's. A temporary foster program was set up while final adoption was scheduled. The family grew in joy and in love. Lisa spent every waking moment thankful for this miracle; this child she had always wanted was now hers.

Before the adoption was final, Lesly's pediatrician began to warn the couple of possible complications. You see, the birth mother had abused multiple drugs during pregnancy and there were medical concerns. There was some indication upon exam that things were not as they should be. There was a strong possibility that Lesly had mental deficiencies. She would probably need special education. The doctor advised against the adoption. Lisa and Bill were crushed and went home to pray.

Why was this happening? Would God keep Lisa from having children, both by birth and adoption? They loved Lesly, of this they were certain, but was the doctor's advice something they should consider before the final papers were signed?

It only took a short while to decide. Lesly was theirs, sent from heaven as an answer to prayer. If there were permanent health problems or mental deficiencies, they would deal with them just as they would with any child given to them from birth. In sickness and in health, Lisa knew without a doubt that Lesly was their baby, and that was all that mattered.

Accepting Lesly for all that she could be, and may never be, they went ahead with the adoption. Less than a year later, the pediatrician declared that Lesly was fine, suffering from none of the mental handicaps he had suspected. In fact, there was a bonus. God had a little surprise in store for Lisa and

Bill. You see, that same doctor now declares that Lesly is gifted. She is a child who will, in fact, need special education, but the kind of education that is derived from advanced intellectual capabilities.

Although the Grefes were ecstatic and thrilled to have a healthy child, they knew one thing: Lesly was a perfect baby from the start, the kind of perfect baby that all children are—gifts from God. Whether handicapped or healthy, they are to be loved and treasured just the same. Lesly is blessed, for her parents knew her true value even before the experts agreed.

Divine Appointment

Sometimes our life brings us upon paths we haven't fore-seen—turning our plans upside down, by twists and turns, until we arrive at the destination that was God's design all along. And so, in 1969, a simple vacation for Cathy Green turned into a lesson that revealed the very depth of God's wisdom.

While vacationing near San Luis Obispo in California, a young and single Cathy set out to have a great time. She stayed with her friend's family on Vandenberg Air Force Base. She enjoyed their companionship and a chance to get away from her all-too-familiar surroundings back home near Sacramento. Life was easy, the beaches were great, and the shopping was even better!

Everything was perfect until the evening Cathy slammed her finger in a door. It was a deep cut, one she couldn't even bear to look at. Since Cathy could not use the on-site medical facilities, her friend wrapped her finger in gauze and drove her to the Lompoc Emergency Room.

"Why did this have to happen now, in the middle of my vacation?" Cathy fumed. She detested hospitals and hated needles even more. "What a way to spend a great week on the coast," she sulked.

When they arrived, Cathy noticed how small the facility was. Since this was the only hospital for miles, it would just have to do. At the door, things just didn't look like a normal emergency room. They rang a bell, and after what seemed like forever, a nurse came to the window, buzzed them in, and began to triage Cathy's wounds. While the nurse was taking Cathy's vitals, a young and desperate woman came racing to the window. She buzzed frantically, and the nurse, right at Cathy's side, stood up to help her.

As the woman entered the building, Cathy knew this was a genuine emergency. The woman began screaming that her baby had choked and wasn't breathing. The nurse rushed the infant to the back, and within a half hour reemerged carrying a healthy, happy baby. The relieved mother was truly grateful. She thanked the nurse, and then she thanked God. And so did Cathy.

All of a sudden, the big picture came into focus. God has a plan; He always has a plan. Cathy would be fine, her vacation only temporarily interrupted. She knew she was at just the right place at just the right time. If she had not been there at that very moment, the nurse would never have been so readily available; the woman would have had the same long wait that Cathy had experienced. Instead, there she was, within seconds of the door, in the perfect position to take the baby and save his young life.

Cathy never looked at inconveniences and setbacks in quite the same way again. For her, they are part of the plan, part of God's perfect design. For Cathy, even a seemingly ruined vacation might be nothing more than a divine appointment with God, an appointment that not only she, but also a young mother and baby, are glad she didn't miss.

A Teacher at Heart

Karen Taylor has a giving heart. In the late 1990s, she decided to make a change in her life. To bless others, she would teach a catechism class at her local parish. Karen was determined to reach out with compassion to help her young students understand God's love.

Intentions being well and good, it was her first assignment, and Karen began to fret. She'd never had children of her own and wasn't sure she'd be able to connect. Karen was fifty-two, and she was concerned about her age. Would this generational difference affect the way she related to these second graders? What if she wasn't comfortable? What if it showed?

Fears began to surface about wanting to fit in and trying to relate to those who are younger. What did these insecurities mean? Karen didn't have the answer, but she knew the One who did. So she began to pray. Karen asked God to help her bond with the children, to accept and to love them. She asked that her age would not have a negative impact on their young hearts.

Finally, her time to teach arrived. The students filed in, awkward and shy, nervous and giggly. She wondered how she'd feel about them. But when Karen looked into their eyes, she realized her prayers had been twisted, turned about in a way that reflected her own needs and not those of the young students in her care. Then Karen prayed differently. This time, she asked God to help the children feel comfortable and not the other way around.

More and more, her heart began to melt, until Karen knew her concern for the children was genuine and true. She shared God's love and the teachings of their church. The children listened with wide eyes and open hearts to stories of Noah and the Ark, of Abraham, and of the Christ child in the manger. The young students were mesmerized as Karen demonstrated each Bible story

with colorful cardboard characters. Touched by their gentle, atten-
tive presence, she was sure that God had answered her prayer.

But He also answered another prayer. One afternoon at the
grocery store, Karen ran into the grandmother of one of her
seven-year-old students. "Oh, Brandon just loves you!" she said
with a wink. "He thinks you're wonderful. In fact, when I asked
him if his teacher was young, he replied, 'No, my teacher is old,
but she is nice.'"

"There it was," Karen thought. "All my fears were in vain. I
may be old, but I am nice." And her students love her still.

Oh, Holy Night

Christmas was over. The lights, the brightly colored packages, even the magic in the air had disappeared. There was nothing left to do but dismantle the decorations one by one and move reluctantly toward the new year. How I loved to keep Christmas close to my heart for as long as possible. But with all the preparation, planning, and excitement, it had ended two days before, even more quickly than I had anticipated.

It was December 27, 1998, and I dutifully went to work as a clerk in the local emergency room. I had been employed at the hospital for almost 10 years. It was always hard to leave home, especially with my family close at hand, the fireplace lit, and warm cocoa simmering on the stove. The hospital, previously decorated with holiday charm, was back to normal. No more displays of cheer in the lobby; no more wooden manger with the Christ Child laying in a bed of straw.

What I didn't know was that Christmas was coming to the ER two days later than usual. My coworker and I sat firmly in our faded blue office chairs, fingers tapping on the terminal keyboards, pounding out one registration after another. We had done this a thousand times before, each patient blending into the next, a constant whirlwind of activity. Only this time, on this night, things were different. As I called my first patient to the desk, I gazed upon a young Hispanic baby named Jesus. Although I knew that in the Hispanic culture the name is most common, I was still taken aback by the night's close proximity to that sacred day. I quietly mentioned little Jesus to my coworker. She flashed a broad smile, winked, and then mentioned that her patient's name was Joseph.

We laughed at the coincidence until a parade of post-Christmas patients began to emerge. Following Jesus and Joseph was an older woman named Mary, then Luke, Matthew, Noah,

Zacharia, and finally a lovely toddler named Angela, whose family had nicknamed her Angel.

At one point, we joked about the possibility of Moses leading his people, staff in hand, through the center of the lobby, right toward our desk! Eventually, after all patients were taken care of, it was time to go home. As we walked through the parking lot, we tried to take it all in. What was the purpose of this magical night? Was it some sort of heavenly sign, and if so, what was its message? Neither of us had the answer, and to be honest, I'm still not sure. But perhaps it is as simple as this: the miracle of Christ's birth is always present, at Christmas time and all year through, if we're only willing to open our hearts and receive Him.

Three Men in White

Patrick is a wonderful husband. He is kind, considerate, and gentle in nature. We have been happily married for more than 14 years. But on occasion, our tranquil lives were interrupted by Patrick's terrible nightmares. Not just your run-of-the-mill bad dreams, but earthshaking, peel-yourself-off-the-ceiling nightmares, medically referred to as "night terrors." Patrick had experienced them since he was a young boy. They came uninvited to haunt him in the middle of his sleep, oftentimes occurring several nights in a week.

In 1982, before we married, Patrick's aunt suggested he ask Jesus to protect him from the horrible dreams. At the time, he had not accepted this faith as his own, but it was worth a try. Anything was worth a try. And, to his surprise, the nightmares virtually ceased.

Over the years, they reoccurred only a few times a year, perhaps to remind Patrick that his strength lies in God alone. When he did have these dreams, I would quickly shake him, rousing him awake and saying a heartfelt prayer. That is, until one late winter night when the angels took over.

It was 1996, and while we both slept comfortably in our bed, Patrick suddenly began to yell. Without a moment's hesitation, I knew instinctively what to do. I started to jump up and shake him awake. Then that still, small voice inside me, the one I have come to know over the years as the voice of God, said, "Leave him alone." It made no sense, but I felt compelled to do it anyway. I remained quiet as he stopped yelling, and a hush came over the room. Pleased that everything seemed to be fine, I fell back asleep beside him.

The next morning, Patrick told me exactly what had occurred during the sacred night before. He remembered having a nightmare in which he felt terrified, almost paralyzed, about what to do. Then, for the first time in this recurring dream, the images began to change. This time he saw three men in glowing white robes standing on a river bank. The man in the middle looked up at my husband and tenderly smiled. In that instant, the tension and horror of the dream immediately stopped.

Now, with these horrific night terrors no longer a part of our lives, I understand all too well. As much as I like to fix things, to hold them in my control, God doesn't need me to intervene at all. He is in charge, and on this occasion, He reminded us both, once again, that true healing, protection, and answers rest only under the care of His magnificent wings.

The Angel in Denim

For Debbie Wilson, 1990 was a difficult time, a lonely experience with much sorrow to sort out and then attempt to move on. Debbie had always been close to her father, who had recently died of cancer. He was a good man, a wonderful husband to Debbie's mom, and a great daddy to his three adoring daughters. Debbie had fond memories of quiet summer afternoons, sipping cool drinks and sharing secrets from their hearts. Hers was a father who understood the importance of family relationships. How Debbie missed him.

When he died, the entire family was devastated. Although Debbie knew he had gone on to be with God to a restful place with no pain or sorrow, her heart still ached. It's never easy to lose a parent, but one so close, one so deeply loved by everyone, made it that much harder for her to go on. But for the sake of her family, go on she must.

One month after her father's death, Debbie's life began to take on traces of normalcy. On this particular day, she made a trip to the local grocery store to stock up on basic supplies. She drove, as if on automatic pilot, parked her car, and slowly walked into the store. This was the last place Debbie wanted to be, but she knew such mundane tasks needed to be done. What she really wanted was to spend more time with her father, but that was impossible. Life had dealt them this hand, her time with her dad was over, and nothing could take that back.

As she entered the store, Debbie caught a glimpse of a nearby vending machine. It was a hot, muggy day, and a cool drink was just what she needed. She placed her money in and pushed the corresponding button, but, much to her frustration, nothing came out. Debbie helplessly pressed the button again and again, until a man behind her quietly said, "Here, let me try." And try he did.

Only this time, for this man, the soda complied, dropping out of the machine as if somehow on command. The kindly gentleman handed the cool drink to her and simply said, "Enjoy."

As she gazed at him, Debbie was struck by the similarity between this man and her father. They were both the same height, boasting a golden tan and possessing a beautiful full head of gray hair. Each of them had the same warm smile and gentle voice. He even wore her father's signature outfit—a white V-neck T-shirt and faded blue jeans. She thanked him and then they went their separate ways.

Later, while pushing a cart down the aisle, she ran into the man again. This time, they struck up a conversation, and the gentleman explained that he was a priest from a faraway parish, in town only to visit his sick mother. They spent about 30 minutes talking, laughing and sharing a bit about themselves. The conversation was comfortable, joyous, and somehow sentimental. He did not seem like a stranger at all, but more like someone she had known all of her life.

Soon it was time for Debbie to go. She walked away slowly and felt a hand on her shoulder at the end of the aisle. It was the priest. He smiled and quietly said, "I'll see you in heaven." Debbie was so shaken by their meeting that she left her shopping cart in the aisle and simply walked out of the store in a daze.

Debbie Wilson will never forget that day. In her heart, she believes this man in faded denim was not a priest at all, but an angel appearing in the comforting image of her father. She's sure she'll see her angel once again, on the same day she sees her dad. Debbie believes they are waiting for her in heaven, where all three will enjoy a cool drink and talk for eternity.

Expecting a Miracle

A young married couple, five healthy children, a family complete. Or so Kimmy DePaola thought. With no intentions of having more kids than she was presently blessed with, Kimmy went to her doctor for a birth control system. She chose the IUD, a generally effective method of preventing conception. The doctor warned her of dangerous side effects, including the occasional misfortune of damaged pregnancies. From miscarriage to birth defects, he went down the list. Kimmy was certain she didn't want any more children, so she didn't take the doctor as seriously as perhaps she should have.

In 1987, while attending a family wedding, an aunt asked Kimmy if she were pregnant. With a laugh, Kimmy assured her she was not. But her aunt seemed unconvinced. Not appreciating the suggestion of an increasing waistline, Kimmy glanced downward. No, nothing seemed different. She quickly dismissed the conversation and continued to visit with other wedding guests.

A few days later, God's warning was delivered through another aunt. She called Kimmy's mom bright and early to tell her that when she had woken up out of a sound sleep, the first thought that came to her mind was one clear phrase: "Kimmy's pregnant!"

When Kimmy's mom relayed the message, Kimmy wondered if everyone was trying to make her crazy. Were they bent on making her prove she was not pregnant, couldn't be pregnant? Didn't they realize she had five children already? What were they thinking? Kimmy told her mom she was not expecting any more babies and suggested she pass that information on to everyone concerned. After hanging up, she entertained the possibility of another child, if only for a moment, but then quickly dismissed it. "Back to reality," Kimmy thought.

Sometimes God has a way of waking us up, persisting, and if necessary, almost nagging us into paying attention. He may do this when we're stubborn, not listening, or too sure of ourselves to hear. He did just that for Kimmy. A few days later, a dear friend called her on the phone. "Are you sitting down? I had the strangest dream about you last night. I was with you in the delivery room and you were holding a newborn baby. It was so real. Are you pregnant?"

"Fine," Kimmy almost snapped. "I'll go to the doctor, if only to prove that everyone's wrong." And, she did just that. But, much to her surprise, the best medical advice confirmed what God had been trying to tell her all along. Kimmy was pregnant! The doctor then explained again that the IUD could cause problems for her pregnancy. It could harm her little miracle, and he must remove the device immediately. There was a strong risk of miscarriage. Yet, deep inside, Kimmy knew that would not happen. She finally understood why God had been persistently trying to shake her, wake her up to the knowledge of this pregnancy, before it was too late. The device was removed, and everything progressed safely. Kimmy had miraculously come to the doctor just in time.

Soon her son Tony was born, and a wonderful gift he turned out to be. With every opportunity, Kimmy teaches Tony, and all her children, to listen to the voice of God, to heed His warnings, for He has only good plans in store for all of us. Kimmy doesn't need to be convinced anymore; she needs only to look into Tony's eyes to know that it's true.

In His Hands

Everyone with a dream understands what it's like. It's something you hold on to, fight to keep, and struggle to make happen. It may be a new home, a new baby, or the fulfillment of seeing your talent put to good use. For me, it was a love for writing and a desire to see my work in print.

I enjoyed writing tremendously and found great pleasure in the process. I would find myself wrapped up for days in front of my computer, tapping away as if words were coming almost automatically. However, enjoying a hobby and making it a career are two separate things. I had been fortunate to have a short story published, but everything else I had written received one rejection after the next. Sometimes they were heartfelt and encouraging letters, expressing appreciation of my work, and yet, never a sale.

After three years, in the summer of 1999, I felt my dream come to an end. I realize there are those who hold on much longer, for a lifetime in fact. Maybe I am weak, but I was tired. It takes great strength to go to the mailbox day after day with hope in your heart, only to be crushed by the first letter. It was at this point that I began to pray. I was no longer offering a begging, pleading "Please-God-I'll-do-anything-if-you-help-me" prayer, but a prayer of relinquishment, a prayer with the understanding that only God knows best.

Now my dream was to have God's dream. And my goal was to find out just what God's dream was. I came to this point not because of the depth of my spirituality, but simply because I had run out of fuel to continue on my own.

I asked God with sincerity, no strings attached, what His plan for my life was. If it included the publication of one story and nothing ever again, that was fine. If it involved simply writing for my own enjoyment, that was fine. If it included being published now, next year, 20 years from now, or never, that was fine, too. I simply came to the end of my rope and didn't want to struggle any longer. I realized that on my own, in my own strength, I could never force it to happen anyway. The outcome was beyond my control.

That's when things began to change. First of all, they changed inside of me. I no longer carried the burden. It no longer mattered what the answer was. As long as it was from God, I knew it would be the right one. Surprisingly, instead of feeling the loss of my dream, I felt free, like a giant weight had lifted off my shoulders.

Then things began to change around me. Within a week, I sold another story, and soon another offer followed. Then I found myself in negotiations for the possibility of a book. An editor was interested. She liked the project. Perhaps we could make it happen. While I waited, I felt a freedom in not being in control, not having a vested interest in the outcome. Whatever happened with my writing career was up to God, and it felt good.

While the publishing company made their final decision, I felt assured over and over: "It's all in God's hands." I awoke early in the morning, anticipating an e-mail from the editor. Today was the day I would find out. I must admit that, if only for a moment, the old control, the old sense of panic began to reemerge. I logged on to my computer and said a quick prayer. Before I could read my e-mail, what I assumed was an annoying advertisement appeared on the screen. Only this particular ad caught my eye. The graphics showed two large hands holding a globe. The words simply read, "The whole world's in His hands." And then I knew, before I opened my e-mail, that whatever the editor's answer, it would be the right one. And I believe it was. For it is this very book that was the result of that decision. He really does have us all in His hands.

A Soldier's Vision

Many had fought and died. All wanted nothing more than to see the war end and to safely return home. Pete Presti was no exception. He was a mere boy of 19, part of the army infantry, fighting in the South Pacific. Like everyone in World War II, he wanted to see the hostility come to an end, to bid his buddies good-bye, and to return triumphantly to his loved ones back home.

The military had brought him friendships, a chance to grow and change. There were experiences that made him a better man, that taught him to fight for what he believed in. But no matter how strong his beliefs, there was a sorrow in his heart for the simple life back home and the comfort only loved ones can bring.

Pete grew up in the small town of Loomis, California. His family was close. Their love for each other was strong. But growing up had been tough. His childhood years were tarnished by a whirlwind, a whirlwind caused by the Great Depression. Most folks stuck together during this time, helping each other as they were able. Each would offer what they had: a skill, free labor, fresh produce from a farm, whatever they could give. It was understood that pride and selfishness would get you nowhere. Pete's family had their difficulties, of course, but by sticking close together, working as a team, and making multiple sacrifices, they had survived. In fact, the Depression had not crushed their family; it had made them stronger.

During that time, the Prestis' neighbors, Antonio and Mary, were busy working an olive ranch and raising three children of their own. The two families pulled together, becoming almost as one. Together, they triumphed over the Great Depression. They were so much like family that Antonio and Mary were given the honor of standing up for young Pete as his godparents. They prayed daily for Pete, just as they did for their own young children.

Perhaps the Depression had helped Pete and so many young soldiers like himself to survive World War II. Hardships being nothing new, they were not a group of pampered young men and women. They were strong and determined, toughened by the rough edges of life.

However, that toughness was soon to be tested. While in the middle of a battlefield in the Philippines, Pete found himself in a foxhole. He was afraid. He began to think of more pleasant thoughts. He began to think of home. His mind wandered, if only for a moment, to his godfather, Antonio. It was his birthday, and Pete knew the two families must be celebrating the joyous event together. How he wished he were there. As suddenly as his mind had wandered, an image, a vision, appeared in the clouds above his head. Pete rubbed his eyes. As clear as he could see, the image was the face of Antonio. His godfather had one simple message. In a firm voice, as only a man who had treated a boy as his own son can, he let out a warning: "Get out of that foxhole!" Without hesitation and with the determination of a young man who knew how to take orders, he jumped from the foxhole and landed safely into another. Within seconds, the ditch he was previously in exploded with a mass of ammunition. Pete sat glazed, his face reflecting both shock and relief.

"How did you know?" his buddies later asked. It would be hours before Pete could tell them. Then he began to tell anyone who would listen. He told them all how his godfather, Antonio, a man who had treated him as one of his own, had taken a moment from his birthday to send him a warning, a warning that had saved his life.

Once again it had happened. Just as they had during the Great Depression, the two families had pulled together. They had reached out to each other as if they were kin. Together they had survived once more.

To this day, their bond remains strong. Even years later, after Antonio's death, Pete remains close to his godfather's children, honoring their history, their heritage, and the legacy of a friendship that transcended time, space, and family ties.

The Message

We've all done it. We've all tried our best to fit in, to impress others, to feel that we're good enough. To some extent, it's human nature. We want to be liked and appreciated for who we are. We will, each in our own way, go to great lengths to achieve this level of self-esteem.

Barbara Kennedy had grown up in the 1950s, the product of an upper-middle-class childhood, a happy home, and two wonderful parents. But nobody's life is perfect. And like each of us, she didn't get through her childhood without some damage, some shadows of self-doubt, some insecurities obtained through thoughtless teasing or from comparing herself to others whose lives appeared to be perfect.

You'd think we'd grow out of these insecurities, but most of us never completely do. We learn to put them aside in our minds, to explain to ourselves that we are good enough and that no one's life is flawless. And yet, we will often find ourselves searching far and wide for something to make us feel adequate, to sometimes impress, to receive the recognition that we desire so deep down inside. For some, this may involve buying a new dress, a new car, even a new home, often chasing objects that are many times out of our reach, more than we can afford, more than we even want. Sometimes they are not even purchased for our own enjoyment, but as if to say to the world, "See, I've made it. I'm somebody. Do you notice me now?"

Barbara, in her own way, was going through a similar struggle. Oh, she was not one to buy expensive items that were beyond her budget. She was a sensible woman, one who knew who she was and whose life was not dependent on what others thought about her. But she had struggles of her own. For Barbara, her insecurities manifested themselves during the summer of 1999. Her brother called. For the first time in 25 years, he was coming to California for a visit. Usually, their family reunions took place in his home state of Texas. But this time, things were different. He wanted to stop by, spend a few days, and enjoy his sister's company. Nothing more, nothing less. He didn't want steak dinners, didn't want to stay at the Hilton, didn't want breakfast in bed. He was not planning to count cobwebs or take note of any chipped and cracked paint. He just wanted to see Barbara, plain and simple.

But for many of us, when are hearts are exposed, nothing is quite that simple. Barbara went on a mission to transform her home into a palace. Everything had to be perfect. She climbed ladders, scraped old paint, and applied a new and updated palette. She bought new furniture, redecorated the kitchen, and purchased elaborate linens for the guest room. She fretted about what she would serve for each meal. Would there be enough food, fancy enough food? Did he like spicy cuisine or mild? Barbara worried about every last detail, until she worried herself sick.

One frantic afternoon, while driving to the hardware store, Barbara found herself waiting at a light. She was distressed, knowing that no matter what she did, it wouldn't be good enough. As she glanced at the license plate ahead of her, the letters seemed to speak to her heart: "ULBOK."

"Hmmmmm," Barbara thought. "You'll be OK?" She wished life could be that simple. Then, as the light turned green, she quickly raced forward. A truck passed her, got in front of her car, and then slowed down. This time, a bumper sticker caught her eye: "Do Not Despair." Barbara laughed out loud. Why hadn't she realized it before? Her brother wanted to see her, not her house. She needed to calm down, quit trying to prove her worthiness, and simply enjoy his company.

We each grow and learn in our own way. For Barbara, her lesson came in an unusual fashion, but it was a lesson fortunately learned. Just like the bumper sticker assured her, when she stopped worrying, everything did turn out just fine. And they had a marvelous reunion.

Titus 3

A ccusations. They can be difficult to defend against, especially when you are dealing with someone who is unreasonable, occasionally out of reality, and often violent. In 1984, while living in the Philippines, Cindy Huggins had fought with her husband one too many times. This time would be the last.

Cindy had been married for several years. She had three young children and was a woman of strong Christian faith. She had tried to make her marriage work, but sometimes, when the other partner is unwilling, that can be impossible. On this particular night, he came home and began to accuse her of things she had not done. He was convinced Cindy was seeing another man. It wasn't true, and yet she knew from his history that trying to prove herself innocent would be of no use.

After he stormed out of the house and the marriage came to its end, Cindy began to weep. Why had God not defended her? Why did He allow such harsh, untrue things to be said about her?

In anger, Cindy's heart began to harden. She began to make her own accusations, aiming them at God. She also began to entertain thoughts of having an affair. She thought, "If this man assumes I am doing such things, then I might as well do them." Surely, this was the way to get even with her spouse.

Her faith would never allow her to take such actions, yet in her determination to get even, she began to disavow her own beliefs. Who was God anyway? Was He even real, and if so, where did He come from?

Cindy cried until her eyes were swollen shut. Then she fell asleep. God was compassionate. He knew Cindy's heart. It was not one of rebellion; it was not one of doubt. It was a heart that was broken, lashing out, a heart that simply needed to be led back into the right fold.

While Cindy slept, she had a dream. She saw a bright light and heard a voice, "Read Titus 3." Cindy woke up terrified. She knew without a doubt that this was God's inspired message. But what kind of message was it? Perhaps God was angry with her for what she'd been planning. Knowing full well that her Bible was within reach, Cindy refused to look up the scripture. She simply cried herself to sleep again, hoping that with the dawn of new light, she would forget the message altogether.

As the sunlight shone through her window, Cindy awoke to a clear memory of the voice, "Read Titus 3." She had not forgotten at all. There it was, as if waiting for her to gather the courage and seek out what God wanted to teach her. She hesitated, only for a moment, and then reached for her Bible. She flipped the pages to the book of Titus, turned to Chapter 3, and began, in part, to read:

This is a faithful saying, and these things I will that thou affirm constantly, that they which have believed in God might be careful to maintain good works. These things are good and profitable unto men.

But avoid foolish questions, and genealogies, and contentions and strivings about the law; for they are unprofitable and vain.

Cindy never again questioned the genealogy of God Almighty, where He came from, or if He existed. She never entertained thoughts of doing wrong to get even with another. She knew her life belonged to God and that He had good plans in store for her. And so He did.

Since these dark and difficult days, Cindy has left the Philippines and resides with her grown children in the United States. She's now wed to Tate, a wonderful man of faith. They walk together through difficult times as well as good. They trust each other, but mostly they trust in God.

Cindy knows that God loves her, that He chose to warn her before she wandered down dangerous paths. She will never again fear the guidance of God. And, to this very day, Titus 3 remains one of Cindy's favorite scriptures.

The Gift of Forgiveness

*I*t's never easy to forgive, never easy to let go, especially when wounds run deep. Fear can keep us bound to our hatred. Bitterness can hold our hearts tight in its clutches, until we are open no more to care, to give, or to love. For Ryan Carlson, forgiveness didn't come easily. His emotional wounds were severe. His memory remained in full view as if to mock his very desire to let go.

Ryan grew up in a strong Christian family near Sacramento, California. His family belonged to a faith-filled church that often preached on the power of forgiveness. But Ryan's faith was soon to be tested.

During the summer of 1997, Ryan, 14, was accompanied by friends on an afternoon bike ride. It was a bright, sunny afternoon, and as the boys rode along the tree-lined streets, they hadn't a care in the world. Then suddenly, without warning, Ryan was robbed by eleven local gang members. Their plot? To steal his bicycle, gold chain, and tennis shoes. The gang cruelly took their bounty, but not without first revealing a gun and threatening to harm Ryan if he told anyone. Their plan? To display power, to intimidate, to place fear in his heart. And it worked.

When Ryan found his way home, his distraught family immediately contacted the police. They later discovered that the gang had been on a rampage that day, beating one boy so severely that he had to be hospitalized. The detective asked Ryan if he was comfortable testifying against the assailants. With faith in his God and the encouragement of his family, he agreed, standing firmly on the scripture found in Isaiah 41:10–13:

> *Fear thou not; for I am with thee: be not dismayed; for I am thy God. I will strengthen thee; yea, I will help thee; I will uphold thee with the right hand of my righteousness.*

Behold, all they that were incensed against thee shall be ashamed and confounded; they shall be as nothing; and they that strive with thee shall perish.

Thou shalt seek them, and shalt not find them, even them that contended with thee: they that war against thee shall be as nothing, and as a thing of nought.

For I the Lord thy God will hold thy right hand, saying unto thee; Fear not; I will help thee.

Two of the criminals were apprehended, convicted, and placed in custody. Ryan's family was relieved, but Ryan wasn't so sure. What would happen when the gang members were released from detention? The boys lived in the same town; some of them went to his school. How much worse might it get if they sought revenge?

After the incident, one of the gang members taunted Ryan by repeatedly riding past his home with the stolen bike. Total freedom became a thing of the past. Even with the peace of God, there was a tendency to look over his shoulder, to take extra precautions. One could never be too sure. The gang members had done more than steal Ryan's material treasures; they had tried to steal his peace of mind. And for that, there was no easy solution.

The Carlson family always takes their needs to God. They prayed daily for Ryan's protection and asked God to change the hearts of the young boys involved in the crime. It was not an easy thing to do; bitterness had to be battled, fears had to be calmed, and anger had to be resolved. Yet they knew that, in time, God would heal not only Ryan's memories but their hearts as well.

A few years passed, and Ryan decided to attend a church Bible camp in the Northern California foothills. The landscape was majestic, the fellowship wonderful, and the worship and teaching inspiring. Ryan began to live anew. He felt old burdens lift, fears dissolve, forgiveness return to his heart, and joy, once again, fill the depths of his soul.

With a new spirit of understanding, Ryan shared his faith with two teenage boys who had accompanied the group on their retreat.

They were new to the church experience, and Ryan was not sure how they had come to join him, but he was glad they had. The boys began to share their hearts, asking Ryan questions about God and what the Lord meant to him. He told them of his experience with gang members, how God had healed him of fear and filled his life with love and forgiveness. The two boys listened with intent, then bowed their heads in prayer, asking God to change their lives. When the last "Amen" was spoken, his new friends sat down on a tree stump and began to speak. They revealed, for the first time, that they were members of the very gang that had robbed him. Through Ryan's open heart, these former gang members were willing to trust in his God. Now, no longer enemies, nor lost in a world of anger and unforgiveness, these three are brothers, brothers from the soul, sharing a bond that can never be broken, but sealed by love for all eternity.

The Healing

It's often said that there are no small miracles, that nothing God does is unimportant. When He reaches out in love, answering even the simplest prayer, He displays His compassion toward us in our time of need. We don't need large doses of faith, nor fancy prayers spoken in the King James fashion, but only a sincere heart, a real need, and a trust that God alone is our provider.

Anastasia Lovett knew from an early age who God was and that He loved her. She attended church with her family, dressed only in her Sunday finest, and rarely missed a service. Her priest often spoke of God's compassion, of His desire to meet our needs if we would only come to Him in prayer. Anastasia took him at his word.

For her entire life she had been plagued with earaches. Not just your run-of-the-mill, take-a-little-medicine earaches, but earaches that involved sharp, piercing pains shooting through her head. Her mother treated her with modern medication and with old-world methods as well. "A little Camphor oil to soothe the ear," she would say. Anastasia faithfully wore muffs to protect her from even the slightest bit of cold. But, in spite of all their efforts, the earaches persisted, driving her to tears and her family to frustration.

She had prayed for God to heal her, but her agony persisted. Perhaps God was busy or simply not listening. Perhaps her young, childlike prayers were unimportant. But Anastasia knew differently. She had been taught better than that. Anastasia had heard the sermons: God cares about all our needs, no matter how small. She would wait, and God would come through.

One cold winter afternoon, while her mother was away visiting a neighbor, her father became ill. Her older sister asked Anastasia to find their mother, to bring her home as quickly as possible. Looking at their father and the serious face of her beloved sister, Anastasia didn't hesitate for a moment.

She ran out of the house as fast as she could, forgetting her own needs and forgetting her muffs. Anastasia's only concern was to find her mother.

As she ran, the cold wind began beating at her ears, and suddenly she remembered. Her earmuffs! She had left them behind. Surely, tonight her pain would be unbearable. But she could not stop; she could not go back. Her father was ill; that was all that mattered. And God took notice.

As she ran, she fervently prayed for her father, and then, only after, did she pray for herself. "Please, God, if You will, please don't let me get an earache tonight." And once again, God was listening.

Anastasia didn't get an earache that night. In fact, her faith and sacrifice were so greatly rewarded, she never experienced this affliction another day in her life.

Anastasia knows God cares for our needs. She has learned her lesson well. Now, with many years gone by, if her grandson's ears hurt just a little, she dispenses his medicine and then gets out her bottle of camphor oil and attempts to soothe his pain. But before she does this, she thanks God for His healing power and gentle loving-kindness toward His children everywhere.

The Faith of Another

Faith can move mountains. It can change our lives, brighten our present, and alter our future. Faith can make dreams come true. But what about those who do not believe? What about those who are uncertain? Does God see their heart's desire? Lorna Trute believes this is true.

Lorna had a wonderful husband, Barry, and three beautiful sons: Dusty, Danny, and Andy. They were a happy family with strong values, a good work ethic, and a desire to stick together through thick and thin. But Lorna was not a woman of faith. She was a practical gal, one who thought spirituality an unnecessary part of life.

Lorna adored her three sons, but she had a desire to have one more child, a little girl, someone she could pamper with the frilly things that seemed to beckon her from department store windows. It was a desire she could not shake, one that would not go away. Some might say that desire stemmed from the very heart of God. For Lorna, it was simply an unmet need that she hungered to fulfill.

In the mid-1990s, after many years of longing, Barry suggested they adopt a baby girl. Following the initial excitement, Lorna waded through volumes of documents only to settle on an international adoption agency called "Holt." The agency was reputable and had been around since just after the Korean War. It had been founded by missionaries, a strong Christian couple whose sole purpose was to serve God by placing His orphaned children in loving homes.

However, Lorna soon came to realize that adopting internationally was not an easy task. There was government red tape, family interviews, home inspections, and a restricted budget tightened all the more by new legal expenses. But eventually it became clear that it was all worth it. They received the call; their baby had been born.

While they waited to bring their little one home, Lorna began preparing her infant's room—and a sweeter, pinker room I'd challenge you to find. There was excitement in the air; a precious little girl was joining the Trute family. They would call her Kaitlyn. Kaitlyn Joy.

Finally, the big day arrived. With great anticipation, Lorna and Barry flew to Korea to meet their angel for the very first time. They took one look at her and knew that somehow she was meant just for them, that there truly was a plan, that this was all intended for a higher purpose. All the longing, all the desire, came to fulfillment in Kaitlyn Joy.

Lorna and her family continue to thrive together, vibrant and happy, three strong boys and their much adored little sister. Kaitlyn has become the center of their universe, and when her mother looks into her eyes, she dares to believe in miracles. Lorna sees Kaitlyn as an answer to prayer, yet prayers not uttered from her lips. She sees Kaitlyn as the result of faith, yet faith not of her own. Lorna knows that her beautiful daughter is an answer to the prayers of missionaries long ago. In spite of her doubts, the faith of another has changed her family's lives for all of eternity.

Lost and Found

My little boy, a lost dollar, and a broken heart. In the winter of 1998, when Nicholas Chand was only six, his father rewarded him with a crisp one dollar bill for chores well done. Nicholas was ecstatic. He boasted of taking his bounty to purchase expensive toys at a local department store. His unrealistic, childlike plans made his daddy smile. Nicholas was proud of his dollar bill, perhaps too proud.

The very next day, Nicholas had friends over to play. He had just met them at school, and they had never been to our home. The children played "store" in his bedroom, happy, laughing, buying cans of chicken soup and cling peaches, ringing up their orders on his toy cash register.

When it got a bit late, his friends went home, and Nicholas began to cry. At first I thought he was just sad to see them go. But as time went on, I noticed it must be something more. As Nicholas wandered around his room, looking forlorn, I finally asked him what was the matter. "I lost my dollar," he told me.

"Were you playing with the dollar?" I asked. Yes, he was. They were playing with real money, mingled with pretend. Nicholas had wanted to show them his treasure. He had been so proud. He had thought it would be all right, had never thought to ask.

I firmly told Nicholas that we don't play with real money and that it was probably lost. Then I felt I must let him in on a harsh reality. We didn't really know these children. Perhaps they didn't understand right from wrong. Perhaps they had taken the dollar bill home with them. Nicholas was devastated.

We searched the room, high and low, under the bed, in the toy box, in the cash register, and in his top dresser drawer, where the money was supposed to be kept. It was nowhere. Nicholas's face grew sadder and sadder.

Finally, I left the room, telling him it was no use. There was no more need to worry. After all, it was only a dollar. But he didn't give up. He continued to look, to search deep and wide, and his silent tears continued to flow.

After what seemed like an hour, I returned to his room. "Nicholas, you don't need to keep looking. If it means that much to you and if you've learned your lesson, just this once, I'll replace the dollar. Now, go out and play."

But, Nicholas didn't move; he just looked up at me with his big brown eyes filled with tears. "I don't want another dollar. I want that one."

Now this perplexed me: was he crying about the money or not? I had offered to replace it. What was really bothering my son? Finally, bit by bit, it all came out. Nicholas wanted the dollar his father had given him, the one he had earned. A replacement would not be the same. He felt badly for losing it, for showing off, and knew that he had been wrong. But most of all, just the possibility that a new, young friend had taken the money made him feel awful. He had to prove that was not true.

Even with all my years of mothering experience, I didn't quite know how to fix this one. As parents, we know the world is full of harsh realities, that people do sometimes take things that don't belong to them. Maybe it was time for Nicholas to understand this unfortunate truth. Maybe it was not. We decided to pray, not just for the lost money, but for a broken heart and for friendships meant to be nurtured and protected. Together we told God that Nicholas was sorry for playing with the money. We asked Him to help us find the dollar bill, if it were lost. We offered a prayer of forgiveness to anyone who may have stolen the money, and we asked for forgiveness for ourselves for thinking such a thing if it were, in fact, not true. Then we said, "Amen."

The very second we ended our prayer, Nicholas's countenance began to change. His burden had lifted. He would be OK. Then suddenly, as his smile began to return, he lit up with excitement.

"I think I know where the money is! I think I put it in the pouch inside the toy box." And so he had. There it was, neatly tucked away, safe and sound all the while. God had found Nicholas's treasure.

Those young, innocent children will never know that, if only for a moment, we thought they may have done something wrong. But none of that really matters, because Nicholas had already forgiven them in his heart, just in case.

Nicholas found more than his dollar that day. He found a new sense of faith, and he discovered the power of forgiveness. The dollar bill? Well, it was spent on an inexpensive toy that broke within a week. But the friendship between the boys remains strong to this very day.

The Lesson in the Fish Tank

*B*alance. Sometimes, that's what life's all about. Not too much, not too little. Whether it involves how much we eat or how hard we play, work, or exercise, it's all about balance. The trick, sometimes, is getting that balance just right.

In 1989, while working at a new clerical job in a hospital emergency room, I ran across an interesting combination of individuals. For the most part, they were lovely people: kind, supportive, and hard working. Many became close, personal friends. But there's always one. There's always that one individual who can make us want to run away, make us regret having joined in, whether it's a new job, a school, or even a church. At my place of employment, it was no exception. This woman's goal, it seemed, was to make my job miserable, to make me give up, quit, and run away. Then, it seemed, she'd move on to her next victim. From a roll of her eyes when I asked a question, to a sarcastic tone when explaining even the simplest of tasks, this woman went out of her way to make new employees feel both inferior and unwelcome.

It's not my nature to sit back and let myself be pushed around. Oh, it may have been when I was young. But now, with maturity on my side, I've learned through experience that a bully is a bully, no matter what age she may be. I've also come to understand that I'm worth more than that. We all are.

Even with the firm understanding of the worth that God bestows upon each one of us, I didn't want to make waves. I was the new girl on the block, the new woman at the desk, and I didn't know what my proper response should be. Should I just ignore her, take it for a while, pray and hope she would go away and move on to someone else? Should I lay into her, tell her where to get off, let her have it, and bully the bully in return? Balance—it was all about balance.

It was also about wisdom. So I went to God in prayer. After asking for His advice, the very next morning I began to gravitate to a scene in my saltwater aquarium. A small fish in the tank had been cornered by a much larger fish. He couldn't come out, couldn't eat, couldn't free himself, for fear of his assailant. I noticed, however, that the other fish, also small in stature, were swimming quite freely throughout the tank, unconcerned by the large, menacing presence. It seemed that the bully fish was all bluff. If the others didn't take him seriously, perhaps there was nothing to fear at all. I began to wonder.

As I shooed the large fish away with the net, freeing the tiny, frightened critter, it began to dawn on me. There was a lesson in the tank, a lesson provided as an answer to prayer. It was all about balance. God didn't want me to be like the "bully" fish, cruel, mean, pushy, and offensive, even if it were only in response to another. However, He had no intent for me to act like the tiny, fearful fish, unable to swim, to eat, to live. He wanted me to refuse to allow myself to be bullied, to come out of the corner, to swim, and to never live my life dictated by the unreasonable control of another.

After that day and the lesson in the fish tank, I stood up to that woman. Not with harsh, cruel responses, but simply with a refusal to be intimidated. I was strong, spoke with confidence, and made it clear that I was not afraid. No more glances downward, no more quivering voice. And sure enough, just like the fish in the tank, she respected me and backed off from her stance. We worked together for years and eventually became casual friends. At times, when the office was quiet, we'd sip steaming cups of hot coffee and laugh as we'd share stories about our families.

Today, we no longer have an aquarium. The fish are long gone, the unfortunate victims of a four-year-old's attempt to feed them a special treat from the sugar bowl. But their life lesson remains, a lesson as an answer to prayer, and I continue to live free.

Giving and Receiving

We've all heard it before: it's better to give than to receive. It's not always what we can get that makes the difference, but how we can share, be of help, offer service, make a difference in another's life. For many, learning to give can be difficult, but for some, receiving proves the greater challenge.

In my life, the latter is true. It's just my nature. I enjoy giving what I'm able, never thinking less of the recipient. But, when someone desires to offer a gift, a simple compliment, or merely the purchase of a cup of coffee while friends meet in a local cafe, I have great difficulty accepting. I know I'm not the only one. For some of us, this is the challenge, to learn to receive from others graciously, to believe these are treasures from God, and to simply say "thanks" and go on.

In the mid-1990s, while facing some unexpected bills, my husband and I worried how we'd make ends meet. We are private people and didn't share our burden with another soul. We did, however, take our need to God.

Sometimes, it seems, when I ask God for help, I often have trouble with His answers. I had expected he'd send more work our way or have one of us receive a raise. I'd even entertained fleeting fantasies of hitting the lottery. But God had different plans entirely.

One day, out of the blue, my father offered my husband and me a large check. It was family money, set aside for the future, and he felt we should enjoy some of it now. Simple, it seemed—miraculous timing, some might suggest—but we were not pleased. We couldn't take money from anyone else, not this way, not as a gift with no strings attached. What did God think we were—takers?

After my husband and I turned down the kind offer, we felt rather pleased with ourselves. We were going to make it on our own.

In the dream, I was sitting in a small cafe sipping a warm cup of coffee. From my table, I watched as a famous singer ran past the glass windows away from a screaming crowd. They were chasing her, crazed for anything they could get, a lock of her hair, an autograph, a chance to simply touch her or hear her voice. She ran past them, ducked into the cafe, and hid in the kitchen. Once the crowd had dispersed, she reemerged from the back room and approached my table. "May I have lunch with you?" she asked.

Proudly, I responded, "No." After all, I was not about to act like her screaming fans, users, people who always wanted a favor.

Then she said something I will never forget. "I don't just want to have lunch with you; I want to serve lunch to you."

With that, I was devastated. I couldn't allow her to do such a thing. I was not that kind of person. I would show her I was different, and she would be pleased. But pleased she was not. Instead of showing relief, her face flushed with sorrow, and quietly she put her head down and disappeared into the back room, alone once again. Then I woke up.

After that dream, my husband and I thankfully accepted my father's gracious gift. To this day, it's still easier for me to give than to receive. I can't help my nature. But, whenever I am confronted by the challenge, whether it be a simple compliment on my hair or a cup of coffee offered by a friend, I remember that dream. I now realize that to turn down any gift is to wound the giver. It keeps them from experiencing the joy that their giving will provide. Yes, it's true: it is more joyous to give than to receive. But, receiving is a joy as well.

Heavenly Express

For some, it's souvenirs, collected from each family getaway, to store up as treasures for the future. For others it's photographs, priceless in their intent, the purpose of invoking tender memories at any moment in time. They cast our hearts back to special occasions, sweet and priceless segments of family history. For Kimmy DePaola, photographs of her children captured her heart. She was seen at every gathering, snapping photo upon photo, candid shots, posed shots, any picture she could get. Unlike many, she didn't leave them in boxes under the bed, someday to be put in their proper place. Kimmy displayed each one of her precious photographs in beautifully organized albums and frames scattered artistically throughout her home.

Family meant everything to the DePaolas. Family and faith, that is. When Kimmy's oldest son, Sal, was 19, he decided to serve God on the mission field. He would share his faith with the nation of Chile. Contact with his family was minimal. It was a struggle for Kimmy, but she knew her son's heart was pure.

It was 1999, Sal's twentieth birthday, and Kimmy missed him more than ever. How she longed to see his face, to hold him, and to take his picture. This would be the first time, the first birthday, she could not take that special portrait. Her dream was simply not possible. Kimmy knew that, and yet her heart still longed to do so. As the day wore on and she recovered from her loneliness, she began to go about her daily routine.

When Kimmy checked the mailbox, there to her surprise was a package from Sal. How strange that he should send her a package on his birthday. Shouldn't it have been the other way around? And what of the postmark? The package had been mailed a mere 8 days before. Kimmy knew from experience that letters from Chile took between 10 and 21 days to arrive; for parcels, it was even more. But here it was, a package from her son, arriving in record time. Kimmy excitedly opened it and smiled when she saw what was inside, the perfect gift, rolls and rolls of undeveloped film. She ran to Wal-Mart and anxiously waited for their one-hour service.

As she glanced at each picture, one by one, Kimmy thanked her Heavenly Father. Every photograph, without exception, contained the image of her beloved Sal. This tenderhearted mother was comforted and reassured. Although he spent his birthday in a land far away, her son was all right, he was safe and sound, and most of all, he was happy.

Kimmy believes this timely package was delivered by "Heavenly Express." God had given this mother the desire of her heart—priceless pictures of her son, arriving just in time for his birthday.

God Never Forgets

In book after book, Karen read their stories. Cover after cover, she'd studied their innocent faces. During the mid-1970s, much had been written about children with autism. There was a growing fascination in our culture. What exactly did this medical condition mean? Was it based on the emotional or neurological? Controversy and interest surrounded these children, and Karen was just one more young student caught up in the whirlwind. She was no more than 16 when she declared, "I'll finish high school, go on to college, and study psychology. I want to work with young, autistic children and try to make a difference." Karen's was a pure dream — one, unfortunately, made just for bursting.

When she arrived at college, just 18, fresh, determined, and excited to begin her future, Karen was put in her place by a seasoned counselor. Apparently, every student he saw had a similar dream. Most wanted to study psychology, and many had been caught up in the same fascination with autism. Quickly, without hesitation, he began to set Karen straight. She would need nothing less than a master's degree. Then she would have to relocate (schools for autism were few and far between). Finally, Karen would have to get in a long line of qualified applicants. The competition would be tough. Being young and impressed by his credentials, Karen was discouraged. Reluctantly, she gave up her dream.

Karen chose, instead, to study sociology. Then, discouraged by her broken dream, she left school a year shy of graduation and began to get on with her life. A year later, while looking for a part-time job, she saw an ad in her small-town newspaper. A boarding school for handicapped children had just opened, and they were looking for help. It was close, less than three miles from her home. Karen was intrigued, so she pulled her resume together and applied. Within a few days, she was called for an interview. While the students were on a field trip, the director gave Karen a tour of the facility, a well-structured school with ample supplies, in a lovely home situated on green, rolling acreage. More than pleased with the job responsibilities, Karen confidently accepted the offer of employment. As the director escorted Karen to the door, she casually mentioned, "Did I tell you the children are autistic?" It was as if bells went off all around, as if God himself was clearly announcing, "No counselor with words of discouragement could take away a dream that I have given you."

Karen worked with those wonderful children for more than three years. It was one of the most fulfilling jobs she'd ever had. Two of the sweet young students were flower girls in her wedding. They waltzed down the aisles like little princesses, wearing long, flowing purple dresses. To this day, many of her former coworkers remain close and loyal friends.

Much to Karen's surprise, the counselor was wrong. Dreams really can come true, especially when the dreams are inspired by a loving God who never forgets His promises.

A Dream of Life

A lovely baby, the gentle sound of cooing, the tender smell of talcum in the air. This is every mother's dream. For as long as she could remember, Cathy Bowe had wanted children. She longed to have a baby of her own, to cherish him, to tenderly share her heart. After one miscarriage in 1975, Cathy and her husband were ecstatic when she discovered she was pregnant again. Doctor appointments were made, furniture was purchased, and tiny, sweet outfits were brought home by the bundles. Then Cathy's nightmares began.

The nightmares were always the same. Cathy would be in the hospital. The medical staff would whisk her baby away, not giving her a moment to behold his tiny face. She couldn't understand why, but it was clear that she had no baby at all. She shared the nightmare with her husband, close family, and friends. Each of them assured Cathy that it was just the irrational fears of a mother-to-be, that everything would be fine, and that in time she would see that the nightmares had no validity at all. But, unfortunately, they did.

When the due date arrived, Cathy was given a crushing blow. Her baby was stillborn. Devastated, Cathy turned to her faith to bring her through. Had God given her the dream to prepare her for what was to come? The shock, it seemed, had been ever so slightly relieved by the warning.

Soon Cathy became pregnant again. Yet tears of joy were soon replaced by tears of sorrow. For just as before, the nightmare returned. Three times, in fact, the warnings came, followed by three lost pregnancies.

Cathy was afraid to try again. She couldn't bear another loss, couldn't bear another crushing blow.

Much to her surprise, in 1978, Cathy became pregnant for the fourth time. She prayed, just as she always had, for a safe delivery. Then Cathy had a comforting dream.

In her dream, she was in the hospital. The medical staff brought her a baby, a baby to hold, and this time a baby to keep. Within a month, her son, Ryan, was born, not without medical complications, but still alive.

A comforting dream, a miracle baby—for this, Cathy will always be grateful. Today, Ryan is a strong, healthy, fine young man. He's the joy of Cathy's heart and continues to be her one and only dream come true.

Is Your Hut on Fire?

O ur children can bring smiles to our faces and heartbreak to our souls. Nothing on this earth motivates us the way our kids do. Protecting them means everything; it's a God-given instinct. Every parent understands this all too well.

We had lived in our California home for more than 11 years. Many times, we had considered moving. But each attempt, no matter how sincere, always proved futile. The timing was never right, opportunities never came through. So there we sat, waiting for God's plan and perfect timing. Each spring we'd plant more flowers, put down deeper roots, and wait another season.

It was 1999, and my 12-year-old daughter, Tiffany, had just completed the seventh grade. She had always done well in school: good grades, many friends, a well-adjusted child. But junior high had been a bit tough. These kids were a different sort, with slightly rougher edges. Maybe it was their age, maybe it's just the time we live in, I'm not sure. But I do know that alarms began to sound each day I'd pick my daughter up from school. There were afternoons she'd come bouncing to the car, eyes bright, happy, giggling, having had a wonderful day. But there were also afternoons when I saw fear in her eyes, while I listened to stories of bullying from a small, quivering voice.

My husband and I tried talking to school administrators. For the most part, they seemed to try, but nothing ever worked. Perhaps they didn't try hard enough; perhaps we are living in such a difficult world that even intervention from the principal seems to have little effect on the outcome. We began to consider pulling Tiffany out of school and moving to a smaller town, a quieter, safer area. Now, I know that no town or school is without its problems. We can only hedge our bets, pray for the right decision, put our families in the best place possible, and then hope our children are indeed safe after all. Anything more is out of our control.

We prayed for guidance. Over the summer, we checked into private schools, and we began, once again, to look at new homes. By the end of the summer, a decision had still not been made. Timing just didn't seem to be on our side. We wanted to relocate, but things weren't falling into place. Before we knew it, the fall semester was approaching. Tiffany was entering the eighth grade. We decided to place her back in school, stay in our home until the following summer, and wait for the right moment to leave.

Two days before school began, my daughter received a note at home. Someone knew her full name, described what she looked like, and mentioned the school she attended. This person claimed to be a fellow student and that they'd been enemies the year before. However, this time the threats moved from simple bullying to the unthinkable. This individual threatened to kill my daughter on the first day of school!

That day, when everything seemed to explode in our faces, I logged on to my computer to read my e-mail. A friend who knew nothing about the disaster we were experiencing had forwarded a story called "Is Your Hut on Fire?" It spoke of a man who was deserted on an island. He'd prayed for months to be rescued, but to no avail. The man had built a simple hut—all he had left in the world. One day, after fishing, the discouraged man returned to his hut only to find it had burned to the ground. Frustrated and exhausted, he questioned God. "Why?" he said. "It's bad enough that I am deserted on this island. I've prayed for months to be rescued, yet here I remain. Now, the one thing I have to keep me from the elements has burned to the ground. Why are you doing this to me?"

Just then, the man looked up. He saw a ship coming to the shore. They had come to rescue him!

"How did you know I was here?" the weary man asked.

"We saw your smoke signal," the rescuers replied.

The tale ended with the notation, "Is your hut on fire?" My husband and I read the story, and I began to cry. Our hut was most certainly on fire. But perhaps these disasters were not disasters at all, but merely tools God was using to bring our blessing: a new home, a new lifestyle, an answer to prayer.

Looking back on that day, I'm glad our hut burned to the ground. The police were summoned, and an investigation began. Unfortunately, the authorities were unable to trace the note's origins. But we knew one thing: there was no doubt about it—it was definitely time to go. We didn't need to be hit over the head; God had made it clear. He had gotten our attention; it was time to move on.

We pulled my daughter from the attendance rolls that Monday and made an offer on a lovely new home. The area is beautiful, and the community and schools are as safe as safe can be. We'll be moving to our new hut in just a few weeks. God answered our prayers in a most unusual way. His guidance was not what we expected, but the scripture proved to be true: "The plans I have for you are good. They are not meant for evil, but to bring you a blessing." And blessed, indeed, we are.

The Anniversary

"The grass is always greener . . ." We've all heard it before. But how many of us really heed its profound warning? Anita Calloway had been married for 14 years. She and her husband, Danny, had three children and a good marriage. Oh, everyone has their struggles, and they had theirs. But for the most part, their love was real, strong, and tested by time. That is, until the mid-1980s, when Anita began to wonder . . .

She began to wonder what life would be like on her own. Anita had been successful in business. She loved her work and was proud of all she had done. Her family was proud of her, too. Perhaps there was too much pride all the way around. As the attention grew and the praise for her success climbed, she began to think more of herself than her family. Did her husband really appreciate her the way he should? Did she get all the attention she thought was coming her way? Did he kiss her each morning as they both headed out the door? Anita began to dwell on these thoughts until they consumed her entire mind.

The Calloways had a strong faith in God. But Anita decided to put all that aside, when one night she asked Danny to move out of the house. Devastated, Danny complied. Their 14-year marriage had abruptly come to an end.

After that, Anita's problems began to snowball. Her business, the pride and joy of her life, began to fail. Then Anita began to drink, at first just a little, then a lot. Her life was in shambles. But she was not giving up. She was not going back to Danny, not going back to her God, no matter what. She was going to do things her way, and nothing would stop her.

God stood back and let Anita spiral downward. Eight years later, when she'd reached the absolute bottom—alcoholism full-blown, a business lost, and loneliness aching in her heart—she reached out to God once again. Sure enough, He was there, waiting patiently all along. She never felt condemnation. Instead, Anita felt God's arms of comfort, arms meant to heal and restore. She began going back to church, something she'd sworn she'd never do again. And her heart began to sing once more.

A few months later, after missing Danny more with each day that passed, she gathered her strength and called his number. "What would he say?" she wondered. Would he hang up on her? Had he moved on with his life? Was it too late to begin anew? Did he have the capacity to understand and forgive? Anita wasn't sure, but backed up by prayer, she made the call and Danny answered. He was cautious at first, but he listened; he gave her a chance. Then they met for coffee. Anita asked for forgiveness, and so did Danny: Anita for giving up and Danny for not giving her the attention she so obviously needed. And they both asked God for help.

That was more than five years ago. Anita and Danny are remarried now. The wedding took place on what would have been their twenty-second anniversary. Now Anita's aware that life isn't perfect. She also knows that the grass isn't greener on the other side. Danny understands that his wife needs extra attention, and he showers her with that attention on a daily basis. Both of them realize that their strength is in God, a God who put the pieces back together, the pieces of their lives that appeared beyond repair.

And now, each morning, with coffee mugs in hand, they share a prayer and thank God for what He has done. Then Danny kisses Anita, and they both head out the door.

A Prayer of Prosperity

Barbara Davis grew up in an African-American home in Mississippi in the 1950s. She and her family were share-croppers on a cotton farm struggling to survive. It was a difficult life, one that brought challenges and hardships. But it also brought strength, a respect for hard work, and most of all, a spirit of family togetherness.

Barbara's parents were strong Christians. They taught their children right from wrong, the importance of faith and hard work. Together they labored for years on that farm. It was hard, back-breaking work. But it was good honest labor they could be proud of. Together, they grew in faith, love, and commitment. With their strong belief in God, dedication, and hard work, they survived. Still, things were not as they'd hoped. Life was simple, money was scarce, and more often than not, they went without.

Eventually, Barbara Davis grew up, moved to California, married, and had three children of her own. She carried for a lifetime the faith of her parents and shared that same hope with her children. Life was certainly much easier in California. But the struggle for finances never ceased.

After Barbara had spent years working two jobs, she and her family purchased a lovely four-bedroom home in the suburbs of Sacramento. They were blessed and they knew it. As Barbara walked into her home each morning, after working all night, she'd thank God for what He had provided. But her thoughts were never far from her home in Mississippi.

In the summer of 1999, a few years after her dear father had passed away, Barbara invited her mother for a visit. Everyone was excited. They wanted to show her everything—her two new great-grandchildren, the beautiful California landscape, and their lovely new home. When Barbara's mom arrived, she was treated like a queen. She was pampered in every way, ways in which she'd never before been privileged. Barbara went through her home, room by room, and selflessly offered her mama beautiful things—a statue, a painting, a tablecloth. They were much loved items that Barbara had saved long and hard to purchase. She wanted her mother to have a better life, better than she had ever experienced in the past. Her mom was in her seventies, and no one knew how much time she had left. Barbara desired her last days to be special, comforted, and filled with small elements of pleasure.

When her mother returned home, Barbara began to pray. She prayed no longer for her own provision, for she had so much already. She prayed no longer for what she could give, for she had run dry. But instead she prayed that God would take over, provide for her poverty-stricken mama by His own mighty hand, with the riches only available at His fingertips. Barbara was shocked at how quickly God answered.

Within a month, she received a call from her sister. Many years ago, their parents' cotton farm had been denied federally funded loans. Their mother's name was on a long list of recipients owed money by the government, funds long overdue. Barbara gasped when she heard the amount. Within the next few weeks, her mom was to receive a check for $50,000.

Barbara had faithfully supplied her mama with all she could give. Now it was God's turn. "Stand still and see the salvation of the Lord."

God saw the heart of His servant faithfully praying for the needs of another. God heard that prayer and answered in ways Barbara could never have imagined. Of this there is no doubt: her mother will be taken care of for the rest of her life—not by Barbara, not by the government, but by God Himself, who is more than able to supply all of her needs.

A Struggle for Faith

For many, faith comes easily, flows almost naturally, only stops to question when presented with a challenge. For others, faith is far removed, distant to the grasp, and a challenge is what brings it into focus. For Anita Short, the latter was true.

Anita was raised during the 1940s by a mother with a strong Christian faith. She taught her to depend on God for all her needs, no matter how big or small. For Anita, faith was something to be reckoned with no more than two times a year—Easter and Christmas. Her life was just fine without God, or so it seemed.

In March of 1984, right before Anita's fiftieth birthday, she detected heavy bleeding from her bowels. This would be a shock for anyone, but for Anita, with faith so far removed, she had nowhere to turn. Determined she was dying, she became angry at God.

She made an appointment with the doctor; he gave her grim news. Anita had cancer, and surgery was imminent. Friends and family gathered around her, attempting to comfort, to lift her spirits. But it was to no avail; Anita would hear none of it. She was convinced she was dying. It was that simple. In her mind, it was over and done with.

While in the hospital, she was visited by a close friend. Her friend had brought a Bible and began reading scripture about healing. Anita, furious and bitter, asked her friend to stop, then told her to leave her sight and go home. She snapped at the doctor and ignored the nurses. Everyone told her that attitude could make the difference, but Anita didn't care. If God had given up on her, Anita had given up on life.

The day after surgery, while still in the hospital, Anita tried distracting herself with a bit of television. It was close to the

Easter season, and a special was on depicting Christ carrying the cross. Suddenly, her hardness melted, and Anita began to weep. Christ had suffered so much; how could she be so hateful? She asked God to forgive her and told Him no matter what the outcome, she would follow Him for the rest of her life. She asked Him to take her burdens, lift them upon His cross, and carry them for her.

Anita left the hospital a changed woman. No longer bitter, no longer angry, no longer giving up. She left with faith that with God all things are possible.

When it was time for radiation treatments, Anita was afraid. She was afraid of the horrible side effects she'd heard so much about. Anita clung to a prayer that her dear friend had shared with her. Each week, while having her treatment, she would recite, "Divine order is now established in my mind and body through the power of Jesus Christ that dwells within me." Anita sailed through her treatments with no problems whatsoever. She was an amazement to all medical personnel she came into contact with. Mostly, she astonished them with her change of heart, her sudden will to go on.

Soon after, her doctor gave Anita a clean bill of health. Her faith grew, and her love for God was strengthened. Then Anita was tested once more.

Two years later, she found a lump in her breast. Old fears rose to the surface; terror once again struck at her heart. How could this be happening again? Why, after all she had been through, must she go through this once more? Upon examination and multiple tests, her doctor broke the bad news. He was certain it was cancer, and this time, it seemed, lymph nodes were involved. Anita began to cry. Her doctor assured her that together they would see this through. "Where is your faith, Anita?" he asked.

Surgery was scheduled. Prayers went up, but everyone expected the worse. Following the operation, her doctor informed family members that the lab would confirm what he was certain of. It was cancer. Things did not look good. Her family and friends gathered around her bedside. They began to lift Anita in prayer. When the last "Amen" was spoken, the doctor once again entered the room. He looked confused. Things were not as they seemed. There was no cancer. Anita was free to go home.

Anita's life has never been the same since. She no longer lives her life in fear, but instead puts her trust in God. She knows the Lord is able to meet all her needs—past, present, and future. To this day, her doctor refers to Anita as his miracle patient. But Anita knows exactly who performed that miracle. It was the Man carrying the cross, the One who lifted her burdens and took them all upon Himself.

The American Dream

*H*ard work and perseverance. That's what they'd always believed. Good old-fashioned hard work, sprinkled with faith, is all they needed to make it in America. Raul and Margarita Jimenez built their lives upon this foundation. They had been U.S. citizens since the 1980s, coming to this country from Mexico for a better life in California. But they still struggled. Raul and Margarita had never taken handouts. There would be no government assistance for them. They were hard workers with three young children. Raul had a new job in construction. Soon, a better life was on the way. Or so they'd hoped.

In 1999, Raul became ill. With no doctor of his own and insurance one month away, he was afraid to seek medical attention. Raul couldn't afford to miss work, but he was sick, weak, and dizzy. He continued to work long hours in the hot sun, hoping to provide for his struggling family. Finally, one evening when he came home, he knew that he could wait no longer. They swallowed their fears, and with children in tow, approached a hospital emergency room.

They were afraid. What if there was something seriously wrong? What if Raul could not continue working? How would they pay the medical bill? Then they met Esther. Esther was a Hispanic woman who worked in the emergency room. She befriended the Jimenez family, brought them warm coffee, and spoke words of comfort in their native language. Oh, English was not a problem for them to comprehend, but somehow her words, in their native tongue, became gifts of life to this young couple. Esther assured them that Raul would be all right. The doctor was a good one; he would find out what was wrong. They began to have peace.

They talked of their faith, and Esther shared hers. Yes, they knew God could take care of them, believed He would meet their needs, believed He understood.

Upon examination the doctor's concern grew. He ordered multiple tests. He needed to rule out the possibility of a brain tumor. The young couple panicked. Between patients, Esther would return to Raul's bedside to reassure him of God's goodness. Her heart melted for this family. Esther felt they'd met for a higher purpose.

When all tests were finished, the doctor emerged with good news. Raul had an inner ear infection, a relatively easy diagnosis to treat. The couple was ecstatic. Raul was free to go back to work.

But Esther did not forget her new friends, and they did not forget her. The next day, Margarita invited Esther to dinner. Their desire was to thank her in the only way they were able, a home-cooked meal, prepared with love and offered as a gift of gratitude.

The next night, Esther arrived at their small Sacramento apartment and tenderly greeted her two friends with a hug. While the children danced around her feet, the new friends sat on the patio next to a makeshift table. Esther was crushed by the condition they were living in—the windows were broken, there was no air conditioning, and they had little furniture. But in spite of their limited resources, Margarita kept her home as clean as a whistle. They were doing their best, yet this was all they had to show for it.

The next day, Esther could not get them out of her mind. She called her minister's wife, Marta. Esther told her of the young family's plight, of their life of destitution, and how her heart broke with compassion for them. The dear woman of faith listened intently. Then she said, "Give me a few minutes. I'll call you right back." When she did, Marta came equipped with a plan. They would gather people together, parishioners from their church, friends that they knew, and they would give, each as they were able, to provide for the family God had sent their way.

The next thing Raul and Margarita knew, Esther was bringing them furniture, linens, pots and pans, lovely dishes, and beautiful clothing. Nothing donated was tattered or old. Instead, they were fine items, items fit for a king. The Jimenez family had never owned such things and couldn't quite believe what was happening.

Within a month, Marta had found them a lovely, new apartment. She had even arranged with the landlord to lower the rent and to waive the deposit. They were going to live in a real home with air conditioning that worked, and with the winter soon to come, a heater to keep their children warm.

This was more than they'd hoped for or imagined. They'd never asked, not anyone, not even God Himself. They were going to make their dream come true by hard work alone. But God had heard their silent cries. He had seen their plight, and He provided everything they needed.

Each Sunday morning, along with their friend Esther, the Jimenez family faithfully attends church. The entire congregation sticks together, bound by faith and committed by love. Raul and Margarita have come to realize that the very illness that looked as if it would destroy their American dream was the very thing God used to fulfill it.

A Bedtime Prayer

*E*veryone who has a pet knows what it's like. A special animal can become like a family member, someone to protect, care for, and love. Sweet, tender puppies, soft, fluffy kittens—they come to us like infants and then grow in closeness as we nurture them day by day. For my 12-year-old daughter Tiffany, her pets—a gray mixed-breed dog, Brandy, and a beautiful black cat, Prince—became her dear friends. She watched over them, fed them, and made sure they came in each night. Then she would shelter them in her room.

In 1998, on a winter night, her cat cried continually and scratched upon the door. He wanted out; that was clear. He did this on occasion, prompting Tiffany to get up and place him outside. However, on this night it was extremely cold—raining buckets, in fact—and being a good custodian, Tiffany knew better than her cat. She tried to shhhh him, but to no avail. She debated whether to give up and put him out anyway.

As she rose to let him out, Tiffany decided to try one more option. Didn't God care about everything that concerned her? Would He even care about a restless, stubborn cat? It was worth a try. She looked at her noisy companion and said a quick prayer: "God, please help Prince to go back to sleep. I'm tired, and I don't want to put him out in the cold." With that, Prince cocked his head and let out one final "Meow" for the road. Then he walked over to her stuffed animal collection and instantly fell asleep.

Together, they slept through the night—her dog cuddled beside her and her cat snoozing upon a soft, stuffed menagerie. Tiffany rested peacefully upon her bed, this time with a new awareness: God cares about everything that concerns us, even about naughty cats named Prince who refuse to acknowledge their bedtime.

The Doubt

Maybe it was the season: the bright-colored lights, the Christmas music on the radio. Perhaps it was a spirit of giving in the air; surely, that's what the holiday was all about. Maybe it was God asking me to do the right thing. I wasn't sure. But in December of 1993, God put my faith to the test.

There before my desk, the stranger stood, surrounded by three young, crying children, just five days before Christmas. As he waited in the medical clinic to have his youngest child treated for a cold, we began to talk. His wife, the children's mother, was admitted to the hospital. She was ill, and to make matters worse, she had been raped the month before—the tragic victim of an evil man. The father was trying his best to keep his family together, take care of the young children, and hold down a low-paying job. It was a struggle, that was clear.

While we spoke, I had contrasting visions of my own children, sitting at home with their father: fireplace roaring; hot cocoa mugs with marshmallows—not too big, not too small—held by tiny hands; a beautiful Christmas tree, illuminated with ornaments, glowing near them in the room. Now that was the way Christmas was supposed to be. This family just didn't look the part. They were clearly outside the loop, struggling at best to maintain some sort of dignity, some sort of reflection of the season—if only, for the moment, they could hold it together. Tears began to well up in my eyes.

I quietly excused myself, went to the back room, and called my husband, Patrick. I told him who was standing in the waiting room. I mentioned the children's faces and a Christmas about to be lost. I asked him if our budget could spare a check, a few hundred dollars. Was it the right thing to do? Patrick, God love him, replied without hesitation, "Of course. If we've got it, write the check. We'll be fine."

Then I pulled the man aside and, I'm ashamed to admit, began to drill him. "If I give you this money for your children's Christmas, you won't spend it on drugs, will you?" He assured me he would not; he hadn't used drugs since he was a teen. He would buy something nice for the kids. He promised. With that, I handed him the check on one more condition: he couldn't tell anyone what I'd done. After all, I didn't want a busload of people appearing at my desk, asking me for money. He assured me he'd never tell a soul. And then they were gone, disappearing into the cold night air, into what I hoped would be a brighter future.

Now and then I wondered if I had done the right thing. Oh, it wasn't so much the money; that could be replaced. But was I really listening to the still, small voice of God? Or was I just a fool, manipulated by another, as he took my gift and used it for wrong purposes?

Several years later, while working in the same clinic, a man sat in the lobby with his young children. He walked up and handed me a note. My eyes flashed across the word *money*, and at first I thought I was about to be robbed. As I read further, tears filled my eyes. It said, "Are you the lady who gave me the money many Christmases ago and asked me not to tell anyone?" It was him! I had not recognized the family at all.

"Yes," I quietly told him. His note intended to keep his promise. He would not speak out loud of the gift, even after all these years. He continued to keep the secret. He was good to his word. We went to a quiet corner and began to talk.

"Why had you done it?" he asked.

"I'm not sure," I said. "I just felt like it." That, of course, was a lie. I believed God wanted him to have the money, yet I was too embarrassed to say so. I thought the truth sounded a bit over the top.

He told me that life was much better for them now. Then he said something I'll never forget. He wanted to return the money.

He could write a check immediately—God had blessed them so much. Flabbergasted and a little embarrassed that my judgment of him had been so wrong, I refused. I said he could give it to another family, anyone he felt needed help. The money was never a loan, just a gift. But it meant so much that he'd offered to repay me; it spoke so highly of his integrity.

They left that day with a happier perk in their step. I watched them go with a different song in my heart. God had been right all along. They were to be trusted; my doubts had been wrong. It really was the right thing to do.

Wherever you are today, if you should happen to read this story, I apologize. I apologize for answering your question falsely. I didn't give because "I felt like it." I gave to you because God is wise, and He wanted you to have it. God never doubted you. I'm sorry I did.

Miracle in the Dentist's Chair

How we long to shelter our children from pain, both emotional and physical in nature. Of course, this is impossible. But as parents we have attempted this since the beginning of time, and we will continue, I'm certain, for always. It was the spring of 1999, and my daughter Tiffany was 12. It was time for the orthodontist to do his thing, to perform his magic, and to send us into debt for the next 24 months. It was worth it, we were certain. Like all parents, we wanted our child's bite to be perfect. No T.M.J. for her. We desired a smile that could light up the world. We were assured that was all possible, with double dental insurance, two fat deposits, and regular, conveniently timed visits for the next two years.

We were on our way. On our way, that is, until her dentist informed us he'd need to pull four molars. Healthy molars, I might add. "Couldn't there be an easier way?" I asked. Yes, there was. But it was not the best choice, not the avenue the dentist wanted to take. Try as I might to convince him otherwise, he was determined. In the long run, this was the route to go. Someday, we'd see, her smile would be worth it.

I was not happy. Pulling four healthy molars to make room for braces and future permanent teeth seemed a bit extreme. I didn't want my daughter to go through unnecessary pain; no mother would. I began to pray. Her appointment for the first two extractions was in four weeks. There was time—time for God to intervene—but how?

I placed Tiffany's molars at the top of my prayer list, just above a book deal and the temporarily missing cat. One afternoon, a week before her appointment, I was watching a Christian television program. While in prayer, the minister began to speak: "This may sound rather strange, but there's someone out there praying about molars. You've been given a bad report from the dentist. Don't worry, God is taking care of everything." I was completely astonished. Could he be referring to my prayer? How could he know?

The next day, while on a short walk with Tiffany, I shared what I had heard. Not wanting to disappoint her if no miracle were in store, I hedged my bets. I explained that all we could do was pray, that God knew her needs. He could choose to stop the dentist from pulling her molars, or He might just comfort her during the surgery. I also explained that sometimes we think God has a message for us, and it's simply not so. I didn't want Tiffany's hopes up too high, and her faith possibly dashed. Yet I wondered, "Could it be true?"

The next week, we went in for Tiffany's appointment. The dentist beckoned me from the lobby and asked that I come into his office. "What now?" I wondered. He explained that the assistant had just taken X-rays of Tiffany's teeth. All four baby molars had no permanent teeth underneath them. The buds should have been there, but they simply were not. Tiffany was just one of those unusual individuals who would never get permanent replacements. Therefore, he could not remove the ones she had. He would just have to do her corrective work another way, be more creative, come up with another plan. I couldn't contain my excitement and told him that Tiffany and I had prayed just such a prayer. He smiled and said, "Well, it looks like somebody up there is listening."

My daughter's had her braces for several months now. She smiles, with a full metal mouth, from ear to ear. Tiffany realizes, as well as I do, that God answers prayer. She knows He cares about every detail of her life, and so, now it seems, does her dentist.

Welcome, Sue

For some, business ventures come easily; stepping out on their own is a natural inclination. They're go-getters: driven, determined individuals. Sue Renz has known no other lifestyle since she was old enough to tackle her first job. Over the years, she tried her hand at several marketing attempts. Many of them were moderately successful, but none seemed to be the perfect fit. That is, until 1991, when a friend asked Sue to work for her local welcome service.

Sue was excited. She could finally use her skills at business, while implementing her natural social talents as well. Sue is a friendly sort of gal. It's just as easy for her to strike up a conversation with a stranger as with someone she's known and loved for years. People like Sue. She's trustworthy, and they sense it. Surely, with this business, she couldn't go wrong.

Her instincts were right. With Sue's help, the welcome service took off. New homeowners would see Sue briskly walking up their steps, ringing their doorbell, and offering a friendly "Hello." Then she'd spend as long as they liked, sharing a cup of coffee and listening to their hearts: their joys and sorrows, their questions and concerns. Sue made many friends in her line of work—some for a short season; many for years.

She loved her job, but it barely paid the bills. One morning, a businessman from her church offered to give Sue free advice. While he looked over her portfolio and studied her business techniques, he made some appropriate suggestions. First of all, why was she working for someone else? She could start her own service and multiply her income. Sue had never considered the possibility, but now she wondered, "Why not?" She could begin in a new town. There was no need to be in competition with her friend.

Sue thought it was a great idea! When she shared the plans with her husband, he thought it was a great idea, too. But when Sue discussed it with her friend, she was anything but pleased. Sue tried to explain. She planned to work a different area, an entirely separate business. But her friend's feelings were hurt, and it seemed their relationship would never be the same.

Sue started her business with a sad heart, and as time went on, her welcome service grew. But the memories of the lost friendship continued to haunt her. She made several attempts to make peace, but all efforts proved fruitless. Sue prayed daily about their relationship and continued to wait for God's answer.

After a few years, when financial problems once again reared their ugly heads, Sue wondered if it was time to give up. Perhaps she needed to get a "real" job. Then she received a call from an old pal, Raul. He had no idea of the struggles Sue was facing. Out of the blue, he called with a message: "Sue, God wants you to continue the work He has given you. Some people sow; some people reap. You're going to reap where others have sown."

A few days later, her old friend called to talk. Would Sue meet her for coffee? Of course she would! Sue was so anxious to make peace, she would have gone anywhere if she thought it would help.

The two sat down over a steaming cup of coffee and began to reminisce. Then her friend explained why she had called. She was starting a new business and was walking away from the old. She felt God wanted Sue to have her territory. She wanted nothing in return, but simply offered it to Sue, free and clear. The two women shook hands for a moment, then quickly embraced.

That afternoon, Sue's business was so blessed with additional clients, she no longer had to concern herself with getting a "real" job. With relationship restored and business booming, she continues her work to this day. If you ever move to Vacaville, California, look for Sue. You'll know it's her when she walks briskly up your steps, rings the bell, and offers a friendly "Hello."

Faith Ablaze

ire! Their home was on fire!!! How could this be happening? It seemed like a nightmare. But for Esther Gomez, the smoke-filled rooms—the presence of the intense heat—were horrifyingly real.

It was February 4, 1967—a night she will never forget. When the blaze started, Esther was in bed. The sound of wind and pouring rain had kept her tossing and turning. Unable to sleep, she had gotten up and walked down the hall. That's when she first discovered the fire: black, billowing smoke, a bright red clothes dryer, and kitchen curtains enveloped in flames. Esther knew she had to react quickly. A gas pipe was directly behind the dryer. Surely, an explosion was imminent.

With a prayer of desperation she ran toward her four sleeping children, but she was stopped by a ring of fire surrounding the hallway. How would she get to their bedrooms? Esther got down on her knees in front of the flames and begged God for help: "I have to get to my kids! Show me what to do!" Then she crawled to Danny's room, removed him from his crib, wrapped him in a blanket, and crawled back toward the front of the house.

Afraid to open the front door and allow oxygen to feed the fire, she placed the baby on the entry floor and went back for her daughters. Esther crawled to the next bedroom, picked up her sleeping two-year-old, Laura, carried her on hands and knees, and placed her next to Baby Danny.

Now, for her older daughters, Sylvia and Veronica. For a moment, she hesitated in front of the flaming hallway. "Lord, I'm running out of time. I can't choose which child to rescue. Please help me." Esther moved toward their bedroom, crawling low to the ground, praying all the way. Sylvia, a first grader, lay sleeping peacefully in bed, unaware of the danger all around her. Esther knew she was too heavy to carry to safety; she had to wake her up. Esther made up an excuse to get her daughter moving. "Honey, we are going to Grandma's house," she whispered. "Get down on the ground like Mommy and crawl to the door." Half asleep, and with much coaching, her daughter complied. Together, they had made it. "Wait here," Esther warned. "Don't move. Mommy will be right back."

Esther still had one child to rescue. She crept toward her six-year-old daughter, Veronica. "Oh please Lord, my children are still waiting in the entry. If I die in this fire, they will all be trapped inside. Help me to help them." As she reached her little girl, she repeated the fib about a late-night visit to Grandma's. Together they made it—past the ring of fire, down the hall, and to the entry.

When the whole family was reunited, they ran outside, through the pouring rain, across the street, and to their neighbor's front door. While the frightened family huddled together in warm blankets, the reality of the evening began to sink in. For the first time, Esther sobbed. Then she breathed a sigh of relief and offered a prayer of gratitude. Everything was going to be all right. God had seen them through. The home could be repaired. All that mattered was that they were alive. God had been faithful.

Within moments, sirens were roaring, and the bright red trucks screeched to a halt. Firemen jumped out and began their work.

When the flames were extinguished, the fire chief sat down, took off his cap, and held it in his hands. Tears were streaming down his face. "Lady, I don't know how your family made it out of there. You should all be dead. The house should have exploded. Somebody up there must be watching over you."

Esther wrapped her warm blanket tightly around her. She smiled and thankfully agreed. Yes, God had been watching. And now, more than 20 years later, with children fully grown and grandchildren abundant, God watches over them still.

The Perfect Place to Worship

For some it is a quiet place, with incense burning and bells chiming. For others, it's a flamboyant minister and loud, intense sermons. For others still, it's modern hymns with scriptures spoken in today's language. We all have our own style of worship. I had mine, but I wasn't sure where to find a place that felt like home.

It was 1978, and after spending several years away from church, I'd just begun to renew my prayer life. Suddenly, I became aware of a need for God in my life, aware of the need to reach out to Him once more. After weeks of quiet, private prayer, I discovered a desire, bubbling deep within me: a desire to worship with other believers once more.

The mere thought of searching the telephone book for a church made me weary. How would I ever find the right one? Surely, most of them were fine places, places where God was loved and served. Yet I had my own personality, God knew what it was. He had created me. He knew exactly where I'd be most comfortable, where I could find a home.

I prayed a brief prayer that God would guide me to the right place of worship, the perfect place just for me. Within moments, I was jolted by the sound of a ringing telephone. I quickly picked it up and said, "Hello." It was a neighbor, someone I'd known for many years. We talked for a minute or two, and then she invited me to a concert. Now I must admit, I was a little annoyed. Hadn't God been listening? Didn't He know I wanted to go to church? This was one night I had no interest in listening to music. But then my friend went on. She had been invited by a classmate, had never been to this place before. The concert was held in some sort of church building. Did I want to come along, keep her company, protect her from religious fanatics? I laughed, got the hint from God, and told my friend I'd gladly accompany her.

We went to the concert that night, a gospel concert, in fact. It was wonderful: the lively music just what I enjoyed; the worship right up my alley; the sermons easy for me to understand; the parishioners with so much in common with me.

If I had searched for months, I would never have found a church so perfectly suited for me. God used an unlikely individual to bring me to a place I could call home. My friend? Well, to put it politely, she hated the concert and never set foot in that building again. And as for me? It's been more than 20 years now, and I still call that place of worship my own. God really does work in mysterious ways.

They Gave Her Brenna

*H*igh school: English exams, pep rallies, football games, best friends that last a lifetime. Anna Carney attended Northern California's Bella Vista High during the mid-1970s. She was an outgoing girl, vivacious, an excellent student and a friend to many. During those fun years, she participated in song leading, rallies, games, and cheer. That was where she first met him. His name was Francis Joseph, but everyone called him F.J. Anna would soon call him a friend.

F.J. and Anna were acquaintances in high school — nothing serious — just a casual relationship, plain and simple. F.J. was a good guy, and a remarkable football player. Anna was busy with a million activities and countless friends. Their lives rapidly moved in different directions.

After high school, Anna and F.J. didn't see each other for years. They each stayed in touch with many high school chums, but somehow had lost touch with each other. Their song leading /football days were over: no more pep rallies to attend, no more reasons to get together. Or so it seemed.

More than 15 years later, Anna and F.J., at a casual get-together with a mutual friend, met again. Old stories re-emerged; old friendships revived. Almost immediately, they began to date, and they fell in love in record time. Why hadn't they connected before? Why had they wasted so many years apart? Perhaps, back in high school, they had simply been too young, too immature, too preoccupied to realize what a perfect match they obviously were.

Within months, they were married. Two people couldn't have been happier. Their families had so much in common. Their friends were so cohesive. Their relationship was so close, so bonded, that they became inseparable. They were truly a match made in heaven.

In time, Anna discovered she was pregnant. Ecstatic, the couple prepared for the much anticipated birth. It was all too good to be true. They had reconnected after so many years, and now they were to be blessed with a child. F.J. and Anna were grateful to God for all of His goodness.

When their baby daughter was born, they named her Brenna. A beautiful infant, perfect in every way, the joy of their lives. When F.J. first saw his tiny daughter, his God-given instincts kicked in. F.J. knew, without a shadow of a doubt, that He would protect her at any cost. When Anna first gazed at her innocent, sleeping newborn, she stopped, took a moment, and thanked God and F.J. for giving her Brenna.

Brenna and F.J. were inseparable. It was clear that she was a daddy's girl all the way. Her smile, her personality, were definitely F.J.'s. One look at her father's baby pictures made it all too clear. They were obviously cut from the same cloth, two of a kind, bound together by love.

One evening, just a few months shy of Brenna's second birthday, the family was returning home from a visit with relatives. They were taking separate cars. Brenna, without question, always rode with her father. She would cry until she got her way; nothing would stop her. But this time F.J. insisted she go with Anna, and Brenna, for the first time, complied. They quickly waved good-bye and jumped into their vehicles.

In a moment it happened. So quickly that, to this day, Anna is still not sure how F.J.'s car was hit. The accident dealt a fatal blow. Before she could hardly take a breath, it was over. F.J. was gone forever.

The funeral was a blur, a stunned part of Anna's reality. Countless friends from their old high school arrived for the services. Friends, even after all those years, came through for Anna and for F.J's little girl.

Anna is grateful for the time she had with her husband. Even though short, the moments were priceless. She is forever indebted for Brenna's safety. Their daughter had been spared that fateful day. She will treasure her forever, treasure her with enough love for both of them. Anna will always be thankful for F.J.'s God-given instinct to keep their daughter out of his car that day, to protect her at any cost.

Now, as each night goes by, when Anna gazes at her innocent, sleeping child, she stops, takes a moment, and thanks God and F.J. for, once again, giving her Brenna.

A Girl's Best Friend

Wagging tail, fluffy snow-white fur. Kajal was Premila Carleson's pride and joy, a young girl's best friend, a beautiful American Eskimo dog. Premila had raised her from the start: Premila, only six years old; the puppy, fresh from birth.

Over the years, they were inseparable. As they played together, Kajal, in full run, approached Premila like a long-lost friend. She'd jump, then tenderly place her head in Premila's lap. It was a priceless relationship, one that brought joy to Premila's heart and a smile to her face.

In the summer of 1999, when Premila was 13, she noticed that her friend Kajal seemed weary. Her stomach appeared swollen; things just didn't look right. Premila ran to her mother for help, but her concerns were dismissed. "I'm sure she's just resting; she'll be fine. Don't worry." But she was not fine.

Within a few weeks, it became obvious that something was terribly wrong. Kajal was not eating as she should, her stomach continued to swell, and she grew weaker by the day. At Premila's insistence, her mother brought Kajal to the vet. Unfortunately, the young girl's instincts had been right, and the vet had bad news. Kajal had an inoperable tumor; she had only a few months to live. They were to take her home and nurture her with love; there was nothing more they could do. Premila was devastated.

As Kajal grew weaker by the day, Premila began to withdraw in sorrow. This was her best friend. They had stood by each other for years, and now she was about to lose her.

A few weeks later, Premila's mother received a call from the vet. She had a dog, a beautiful American Eskimo, who needed a home. The poor animal had been injured, hit by a car, and was paralyzed in one leg. The vet had called everyone in search of help.

Premila's family was her last hope. The next step for the disabled dog was the shelter, where this sweet, innocent canine was sure to meet her death. The vet knew it was a difficult time for the family, so close to losing their beloved pet, but could they take this injured dog in? Could they give her a home?

With only a moment's hesitation, they agreed. Soon after, the vet drove the dog to her new home. When she arrived, Premila's mom was given a warning. The pooch had been through so much—an accident, surgery, lost and alone—she was not friendly. She would go to no one. It would take time to gain her trust. Premila's mother approached the dog slowly, patted her soft, furry white head, and then offered her a bowl of cool water. The wounded animal seemed nervous, afraid, shaky, and distant. She was not about to get close to anyone.

Within moments of the dog's arrival, Premila burst through the door. She caught a glimpse of the beautiful dog. For the first time in weeks, the young girl began to smile. Without hesitation, the wounded dog approached Premila in full run, as if she had just seen a long-lost friend, jumped, and then tenderly placed her head in Premila's lap. Healing, for both, had just begun.

On the Wings of a Dove

*A*nita Calloway felt desperate. Her concern grew with the dawn of each day. It was the summer of 1999, and her lovely grown daughter, Danita, had just moved with her family to California. Now she was about to make a two-week trip back to Seattle to wrap up loose ends. For Danita, this was a necessary journey to a difficult territory—a place where she did not feel welcome—and she did not want to go.

Danita and her family had moved to California to address her son's learning disability. In Spokane, Danita had hit every roadblock imaginable in search of an appropriate special education program. The frustrating memories kept her fearful of returning to Spokane, even if only for a short visit. But go, nonetheless, she must. Mother and daughter spent several days before the trip crying with each other and crying out to God.

Mothers want to protect, to keep even their grown children from harm. It is their basic instinct, the very purpose held deep within their souls. Anita was no exception. She pleaded with God to change circumstances, to arrange things so Danita no longer had to go. God could do it; God was able. But God, it seemed, would not answer.

The night before the trip, Anita went to her daughter's home. They cried together; then they prayed. As they hugged good-bye and Anita walked to the door, their eyes first saw it. Resting quietly upon the walkway sat a pure white dove. Both mother and daughter let out a gasp. They had never seen a pure white dove before and certainly not in their own front yard. But there he sat, as if beckoning them to look deeper.

Anita asked her daughter if she knew what a dove represented. Yes, she did. It was a sign of the Holy Spirit, a sign of peace. They smiled and laughed a bit, if only from relief, and then gave each other a hug. Everything was going to be just fine. There was no doubt about it; this was a sign from God. He would take care of everything. He would send his Holy Spirit to travel with her. And He did.

Danita returned two weeks later, a different woman. Things had not gone at all as she'd feared. In fact, her family had had a wonderful time. There were no problems, no bad memories to hound them from the past. They had even taken a relaxing respite, walking the warm, sandy beaches along the coast, as they made their journey home.

Anita realized she's not the only one who has instincts to protect her daughter, whose love for another runs so deep. God showed her that day that His love is immeasurable, His protection sufficient. He revealed His compassion with a sign of peace and of the Holy Spirit, a sign sent in the form of a pure white dove, a testimony of faithfulness resting quietly on the doorstep.

The Adventure

It was a warm summer day in 1980 when two young boys, Antonio, five, and Hector, nine, were making their first short walk to the local convenience store. For months the children had begged for permission to go. But their mother, Marta Marquez, would hear nothing of it. Although the store was just a short distance from their home, Marta knew that careful moms don't take chances. And so the boys had waited.

One afternoon, Marta decided they were old enough to make the short journey alone—but only on strict conditions. First, they had to go straight to the store and then straight back again. The boys were forbidden to talk to anyone, and they were not to stop for any reason. Was that a deal?

"Yes," they promised. They would do as they were told.

Marta reached into her wallet and pulled out just enough money for Hector and Antonio to buy a few pieces of delicious candy. Then she sent them on their way. As they walked out the door, she reminded them of their promise and added one more condition: "I know just how long it takes to walk to the store, buy candy, and return. If you are not back in exactly 15 minutes, I will come looking for you."

"We'll be back on time," the excited boys promised. Then off they went on their first adventure. Marta smiled as she saw her two sons happily skipping to the store. This was a sign of independence, a milestone in their childhood. She glanced at the clock, estimated the time of a safe return, and proceeded to prepare dinner.

While she was making tortillas, Marta felt an inner voice compel her to action. "Your sons are in danger; pray for them!" Marta immediately stopped, bowed her head, and asked God to watch over her children. "Please protect and keep them safe from harm." When she raised her head, she glanced at the clock. Twenty minutes had gone by since the boys had set out for the store. They should have been home by now.

Marta rushed toward the door. But before she could get outside, Hector and Antonio met her on the front porch. "Mom, we're so glad we didn't listen to you today," Hector said.

Marta caught her breath. "What do you mean you didn't listen to me? Why are you late?"

"We stopped in the field to pick wildflowers for you. Picking the flowers made us late, and it's a good thing, too, Mom. By the time we got there, a car had driven through the glass and had crashed inside the store."

Marta embraced her two sons and held them close to her heart. "Thank God, you are both all right." Hector proudly handed his mother a bouquet. Marta's eyes filled with tears.

Upon further investigation, Marta discovered that a drunk driver had crashed through the storefront window only minutes before the boys' arrival. If they had not stopped on the way, Hector and Antonio might have been killed.

That night, as the family gathered around the table eating fresh, warm tortillas, the children excitedly chattered about their day. As they spoke, Marta gazed lovingly at Hector and Antonio. From the corner of her eye, she could see the delicate wildflowers placed with honor in a small, shallow vase. That night, Marta thanked God for many blessings: for sparing her two sons, for little boys on their first adventure, and for her sons' loving, tender hearts. Then she added something more: she thanked God for the wildflowers, a hand-picked gift of love, that brought her a much greater treasure—her children's very lives.

Devoted to God

*P*regnancy: tired, bloated bodies, nausea at the mere sight of food. Labor: intense, painful, wondering if it will ever end. As women, we'll go through anything to behold the face of an innocent babe, a child to call our own.

For Devonne Williams, pregnancy didn't come easily. She had three healthy children. But with each birth she carried distant memories of difficult times, complications she tried to forget. Her three beautiful children were all that mattered. No suffering was too great to have them in her life.

Then in 1998, she became pregnant once more. Fear began to set in as the usual nausea and vomiting grew to unprecedented proportions. She was admitted to the hospital, given IVs, and sent back home, where she often remained bedridden, barely able to provide for the little ones under her care.

One afternoon, when her mother came to help out with the children, she innocently asked, "Devonne, why do you keep doing this to yourself? You know how terribly ill pregnancy makes you. Why did you do this again?"

Devonne, too weak to answer, began to wonder.

One afternoon, without a doubt in her mind, she knew that the baby had turned; he was now breach. Devonne called her doctor to tell him the news. He chuckled, calling her an alarmist, and promised to grant medical reassurance. But when the skeptical doctor examined her, he grew pale. Devonne had been right: the baby was breach! A C-section was scheduled. She was devastated. Devonne wanted desperately to deliver this baby naturally.

A dear friend who worked at the hospital called to schedule her surgery. Devonne recited insurance information, but she was determined that the C-section would never occur. She had been through so much; she was clearly in denial.

For the next four days, the baby would turn, engage himself in the birth position, and then turn again—breach as before. A C-section canceled, a C-section rescheduled. A roller coaster for Devonne.

Early one morning, she received another call from her friend at the hospital. Where was she? Why wasn't she there? Her room was ready. What was going on? Devonne explained that the surgery had been canceled. She was sorry the hospital had not been notified. Her friend said that Devonne's doctor was sitting right next to her desk. He spoke to his patient, told her he was going out of town for the weekend, and asked how she was feeling. Devonne had not wanted to bother him. She had not planned to tell him that the baby was, once again, in the breech position. Her doctor insisted she come in right away; the surgery would be performed immediately.

Devonne reluctantly obliged. Within an hour, she and her husband arrived at the hospital. Devonne was prepped for surgery. From there, things progressively went downhill. During the C-section, her blood pressure plummeted to dangerous levels. She began to code, and emergency measures were taken. Then, just when things began to look brighter, her son was delivered. He did not cry. There was silence in the room. Hysterical, Devonne wanted to know what was wrong. Her baby was blue. He was not crying. Why couldn't somebody help him? A specialty team rushed in. Within moments the color returned to his face, and her newborn son, thankfully, began to cry.

Soon the facts came out: the umbilical chord had been kinked through four days of twists and turns. He had almost died. They had almost lost their tiny son. They named their baby Lemuel, "Devoted to God." Devonne knows that if it had not been for a miracle, the prompting of a friend's call at just the right moment, it would have meant certain death for her son. God was gracious, and their family would be devoted to Him for all eternity.

Devonne now has an answer to her mother's question. Why, indeed, had she done this again? She did it for Lemuel, and Devonne knows that every single moment was worth it.

Roses for Marian

Marian Midboe grew up in the beautiful South Dakota countryside. It was a simple life: hard work, fresh air, lots of love to go around. For Marian, life was good. Her parents raised her and her seven siblings with a strong belief in God. There were prayers at mealtime and prayers at bedtime. And in between, they were taught the true meaning of faith. God was a part of their everyday existence. He was never far away, always available in a time of need.

Suddenly, without warning, their time of need arrived. At the age of 10, Marian was struck with a fever, a fever so severe that her worried mother thought she might lose her. They had tried everything to lower the raging temperature, but nothing worked— not medicine, not cool baths, not even the tender embrace from a heartsick mother. In spite of all they did, the fever continued— blazing, determined, dangerously out of control.

Her mother stayed by her side for four continuous days. She never left Marian's room, even for a moment, afraid that if she did, her daughter might be gone, her precious young child might be taken away from her forever. She stayed beside her, night and day, speaking words of comfort, offering a cool compress for her child's burning forehead. And she prayed like she had never prayed before. She prayed for healing, she prayed for mercy, and she prayed for many more years with her child.

On the fourth night, with almost no hope in sight, the frightened mother heard her daughter begin to moan. "This was it," she feared. Marian was dying. Her daughter was being taken from her.

Then young Marian spoke. "There is an angel in the room, right there in the corner. Mother, can you see her? She's beautiful, all dressed in white, and she carries a bouquet of red roses. Mother, can you see her now; can you see her?"

Her mother saw no one, felt no one, heard no one. She heard nothing but the cries coming from Marian herself. Could this angel be real? Was she there to take her daughter to heaven? Was it too late for prayers of healing?

Then Marian fell asleep. Her mother ran to her, touched her, leaned close to see if she was still breathing. Yes, she was. She was still alive! The angel had not taken her away!

Marian awoke a short time later—fever broken, no longer ill, completely recovered. Her family rejoiced. Marian was going to be all right; she would live! Their prayers had been answered.

Mother and daughter talked about the angel that day and for many years to come. "What did she look like? Who was she? Why had she come?" There were so many questions. Of the little they understood, this was clear: her angel did not come to take her away, but to bring a gift, the gift of healing, sent from God as an answer to prayer. The angel had given young Marian back her life.

Many decades have passed since the beautiful, glowing angel came to pay her a visit. But one thing is certain: Marian will never forget. She has no reason to fear—not sickness, not sorrow, not even the day God chooses to take her home. For Marian knows her angel will return, with roses in hand, and escort her triumphantly into heaven.

With a Twitch of Her Brow

Sometimes, water is thicker than blood. Sometimes, friendships are deeper than family ties. For Devonne Williams, her relationship with her friend Geneva, "Aunt Geneva" as she respectfully called her, was more like true family than most could understand. Her mother and Geneva were best friends. Because of the women's close relationship, Devonne had known Geneva since birth. She always thought of her as an aunt—*friend* was just not a strong enough word. Their relationship was deeper, closer. Yes, they were as much family as family can be.

During Devonne's teen years, she would go to Aunt Geneva and share her heart: her fears and secret crushes on young boys at school. Aunt Geneva would smile sweetly, then gently twitch her eyebrows as if to say, "All is well. I love you." It became their secret sign. Whenever her aunt was pleased, proud of Devonne for something she'd done, she would give the sign—a twitch of her brows, up and down, ever so gently—and Devonne would know she was truly loved.

It's human nature to get wrapped up in ourselves. We all do it, become the center of our own universe. Devonne was no exception. Weddings can be stressful, exciting, intense times. There is much planning to do; every detail has to be perfect. It's a big moment, and everything has to be just right.

It was 1993, and Devonne was marrying the man of her dreams. Her friends, her family, and of course Aunt Geneva would be there. Of this, there was no question. She could imagine it no other way. But Aunt Geneva had not been well. She was having complications from a long battle with diabetes. Devonne knew this, of course, but her aunt, well, she was invincible. She'd be all right. Everything would be fine.

Her wedding day arrived. The flowers were perfect, the dress was everything she'd dreamed of, the music was exactly on tempo. No one tripped down the aisle, and no one stumbled over their vows. Everything went exactly as planned. Except, that is, for one important thing. Where was Aunt Geneva? Devonne had searched the building, eyes darting back and forth, almost in a panic. Where was her beloved aunt? How could she miss the most important day in Devonne's life?

Bitterness set in; anger soon followed. Even when an explanation arrived—Aunt Geneva had been ill, needing dialysis, weak, and unable to attend that sacred occasion—Devonne didn't want to listen. This was about her wedding, her special day. Aunt Geneva should have been there. But hidden deep within the anger and the apparent selfishness was fear, lurking below, trying to come out. Devonne was afraid to hear that her beloved aunt was ill; she couldn't bear to lose her. For now, it was much easier to be angry than to deal with reality.

Devonne didn't speak to Aunt Geneva for more than a year. Why call? Why talk? It was no use; it was done. The wedding was over. No one could bring that day back and do it over again.

Then in 1995, Devonne heard the news. Aunt Geneva was back in the hospital. Things didn't look good. Due to diabetic complications, her aunt had lost a leg. Now, with kidney failure, the doctors had gathered the family at Geneva's bedside to say good-bye. Devonne dropped everything and ran to the hospital. On the way, she frantically prayed: a prayer of desperation, a prayer of repentance, a prayer for a second chance.

The moment she arrived, Devonne saw Aunt Geneva's children. They were frightened; they were crying. Devonne had not spoken to any of them in more than a year. She felt horrible. She had been so selfish, caught up so much in her own needs, she had forgotten about theirs. She knew it was time: time to say "I'm sorry," and time to deal with reality. Aunt Geneva was not invincible; she needed to finally accept that.

The doctor informed Devonne that her aunt was unconscious. She recognized no one and didn't understand what was going on around her. He did, however, assure Devonne that Geneva was no longer in pain, just resting comfortably.

Devonne gently pulled the curtain and quietly stepped next to Aunt Geneva's bed. What she saw shocked her. This woman could not be her beloved aunt! The illness had taken a powerful toll. Her body was so thin, so ravaged by disease, Devonne could hardly bear to look. She bent down low, reached forward, and began to weep. Devonne apologized for being away so long, for holding resentment in her heart. Then she said, "I love you."

Without a moment's hesitation, eyes still closed, Aunt Geneva smiled sweetly and ever so gently twitched her brows, up and down, just a bit. That was the sign! Then Devonne knew that all was well. Aunt Geneva loved her still. Within a few hours, her last breath was taken. Aunt Geneva died with a smile on her face and with her family beside her.

Devonne awaits the day when she'll see her beloved aunt again. She's certain she'll find Aunt Geneva waiting for her at the gates of heaven, a sweet smile upon her face, and then a twitch of her brow, ever so gently, up and down, to tell her all is well—to tell her she's still loved.

Just a Little More Time

A tenderhearted mother, a loyal wife, a woman with a deep love for God. Judy Carlson's mom, Mickie, was all this and more. They were close through Judy's growing years, and now, into her adulthood. Her mama was never farther away than a quick phone call.

Mickie would visit her children frequently, journey across California if necessary, just to be with them. Then they'd sit upon a soft, comfy couch, talking, reminiscing, and sipping warm cups of tea.

In 1991, after one such trip, Mickie headed for home. Only this time she never arrived. Within hours, the family had been contacted. Mickie was in the hospital. She'd been taken by life flight from a serious car accident. Little by little, the details came out. Her mother's car had gone off the road. No one's sure why, but it had flipped three times and landed back on the freeway headed in the wrong direction. Two truckers saw the accident and responded as heroes. They moved their trucks to make a "V" around her car, like the wings of an angel, protecting her from oncoming traffic. A nurse, traveling with her family on vacation, had watched in horror as the accident occurred. She leaped from her vehicle and offered quick and lifesaving medical assistance. The nurse, a woman of strong faith, cared for her patient. Then she prayed: she prayed for the woman's life, she prayed for her soul, and she prayed for those she knew would soon hear the horrible news.

When Judy joined her family at the hospital, the doctor took them aside. The patient had a broken collarbone, broken ribs, and a broken vertebrae. She would probably be paralyzed. It was touch-and-go. No one could promise she'd make it.

Judy prayed. She prayed for healing, she prayed for God's will, and she prayed for more time.

Soon, her mama improved. She was transferred from ICU to the medical floor. Things were looking up. Perhaps she would make it. While her dad was never far from his dear wife's side, spending months camping out in the hospital, Judy continued to pray.

While Mickie was in the hospital, mother and daughter had shared moments together, moments of heartbreak, moments of tears, and moments of love. Judy now offered in return the very love for God her mother had instilled so deeply within her. Then, finally, Judy prayed for God's will to be done.

Suddenly, Mickie took a turn for the worse. Then, without warning, she died—even after all she'd been through, even after months of medical care, even after the miraculous circumstances of her rescue. It was time for Mickie to go. She'd hung on long enough.

Judy still misses her mom; a daughter always will. But she treasures the last moments they had together. No, they did not include afternoons spent on a soft, comfy couch, sipping warm cups of tea. But for Judy and her mom, their last sacred moments together were precious just the same.

A Christmas Angel

Cliff was a special man, a priceless gift. His tender heart, his deep spiritual faith, were qualities that permeated his presence. An uncle by marriage, Cliff came into Kathy's life with a depth that stemmed from many hours in prayer, many hours in the presence of God.

In 1965, Cliff lost his wife on a lonely, gray December day. He rarely spoke of her, but his countenance revealed a love beyond measure. His home was filled with memories, a legacy of her life on earth. Cliff hoped to see his wife once more, in a place without distance, in a time without end.

For many, Christmas brings sorrow: reminders from years gone by, of love long departed. Each December, Kathy would visit her uncle, if only to warm his home with laughter, to drink a cup of soothing cocoa, and to fill his day with cheer.

Many Christmases came and went, each season flowing endlessly into the next. And in 1986, as we someday all must do, her dear uncle came to his final day on earth. Christmas, for Kathy, would never be the same.

Weeks after Cliff's death, a small wooden box was discovered among his belongings. Inside were beautiful poems, revealing her uncle's deepest thoughts, secrets, and emotions. He had written them for years, some to his wife, some to his God, some to the family who would surely find them one day.

A particular poem touched Kathy's heart. Next to the beautifully penned words was an inscription. It read, "This is a true experience. It happened Christmas Day, 1973."

Then a bible quote followed:

Behold, I send an angel before thee, to keep thee in the way, and bring thee into the place I have prepared." Exodus 23:20

Kathy, began to read:

An angel came into my dreams,
So lovely and so fair,
Her eyes were blue as blue can be,
Cascading gold her shining hair

From whence she came I never knew
Nor where she went when taking leave
Tarrying but a little while,
Telling me always to believe

Ever and anon she returned again
In the stillness of the night,
And the beauty of her presence,
Was a softly glowing light

I longed to find this little girl,
And made a sacred vow,
For I could see the grace of God,
Resting on her brow.

Then, lo, one cheerless Christmas Day,
She came to my lonely door,
With a kitten cradled in her arms,
A gift of love forevermore.

So, my dreams weren't only dreams,
But, a vision of things to come,
For she came and stayed, then went away,
And never said where she was from

Oh, to see her once again,
my forlorn soul I'd give
To touch her golden halo,
And once again, to live.

Kathy's heart melted. Her uncle had once received an angelic visitor on Christmas day! As she continued to read, tears began to fall. Kathy was comforted with the assurance that her dear uncle was now in the presence of God, embraced in the arms of his beloved wife. He'd been escorted, hand in hand, by a golden-haired angel—an angel who returned to take him home, where, once again, he lives.

Brightly Wrapped Packages

Each holiday has its special moments, its beauty, its memories. But for me, it's Christmas that sets my heart to music, with crisp air, freshly baked cookies, and three wise men looking majestically into a makeshift manger. Every detail makes the holiday come alive with joy.

In the mid-1960s, when I was about nine, I decided to change our family's Christmas tradition. This was the year everything would be different. I would buy gifts with my own money, no longer relying upon the kindness from my mother's pocketbook. I wanted to give from my heart, from my own budget, without help from anyone. But how could I do it?

Christmas was only days away. I could offer to perform extra chores, but there wasn't enough time, wasn't the opportunity to receive enough money to give the kinds of gifts I had imagined. So, with the faith of a child, I went to my father. My Heavenly Father, that is.

I asked for a miracle. I asked for just enough money to buy presents for my family. One special gift each, wrapped beautifully, of course, with red and green paper, tied up in bright, shiny bows. I desired to make my family rejoice, surprise them beyond measure. I simply asked, and then I said, "Amen."

I can't explain exactly how, but somehow, I just knew. I was to look in the drawer, the drawer of an old maple nightstand kept near my bed. The nightstand was there all right, it had been there as long as I could remember, but I already knew what was inside. It contained no money. Oh, there were wads of papers, notes from friends and my numerous sketches of the "Queen of Stars" (my favorite drawing—a beautiful woman of magnificent royalty, with a long-flowing, sequined gown and a tiara upon her head). That was it. OK, maybe a few sticks of gum, but there was absolutely no money to be had in that drawer. As I sat, I wondered how God would perform the miracle. Would He send a neighbor with a job offer, perhaps a dog that needed to be walked, weeds that needed to be pulled? Finally, with the impulse persistent, I reluctantly opened the drawer and began to rummage through it. Yes, just what I'd thought: notes, sketches of the Queen of Stars (my, she looked good), but what, what was this? Folded together in a small bundle were several one dollar bills. To this day, I can't remember how much, and I also can't tell you how they got there. I can only say it was more money than any nine-year-old should have thrown in the bottom of a drawer, and one I had no accounting for.

Amazed, I ran to my mother. Who did it belong to? Nobody knew. No one, in fact, had known of my prayer. No one but God had told me to look in the drawer. But there it was.

That year, I bought special gifts for my family. I purchased them with money not supplied by my mother, but by my Heavenly Father. I can't remember what I bought, except for one item: a gaudy, gold-painted, metal, filigree hair spray container that I proudly chose for my sister. (Hey, it was the 1960s.) Everything else is a blur. But one fact that's not lost to my poor memory is that God heard the prayer of a young girl—a girl who asked not for herself but for others—and answered with a triumphant "Merry Christmas!"

A Boy Named Kyle

K yle: eyes of blue, sunny blonde hair, a beautiful child. His whole family adored him. He was the middle sibling, with an older sister and a baby brother, each sharing a happy home. Danita Bonser loved her children and knew she would do anything for them. She caressed the young baby, baked cookies for the older two, and prayed for each one as she rocked them to sleep in their lovely Washington home.

In the spring of 1998, around the time of Kyle's third birthday, Danita became concerned. Never once had her son spoken a word. With so much going on in the house—a recent pregnancy followed by a critically ill, then recovering infant—there had barely been time to notice. They had just thought Kyle was a late bloomer. Yet now it seemed there was more to it than that.

Danita took Kyle to his pediatrician. Was there something wrong with his hearing? Was that why Kyle had never spoken? The doctor performed various examinations. No, it was not his hearing, and his lab work was fine, too. Perhaps he would speak soon. Just go home and wait; he'll catch on in time.

But a mother knows better. Danita sensed there was more going on. Determined to understand, she contacted a public health nurse and asked questions. Could someone come to her home? Could the nurse take a look at Kyle? The nurse agreed, came by the house, sat on the floor with Kyle, and performed a battery of developmental tests. Out of a possible 35 points, Kyle received only 3. Then she asked the question Danita will never forget: "Have you ever heard of autism?" Danita had not. The compassionate nurse began to explain. Autism was a neurological disorder that often accompanied delayed abilities and behavioral abnormalities. She referred Danita back to Kyle's doctor.

The doctor was less than enthusiastic in being second-guessed by a public health nurse. But with concern for Kyle, and perhaps to cover himself, he brought Kyle back in for further testing. When the results were inconclusive, he referred Kyle to a specialist.

Eventually, the public health nurse was proven right. Kyle was diagnosed with autism. Danita was devastated.

She spent months on the phone, calling everyone she could to get help for her son. She called social services, the health department, special schools, and special doctors. She fought with the Department of Social Security and with her private insurance company. Danita took careful notes of all her conversations. She has five spiral notebooks completely filled to testify to her frustration.

The tension in her home began to grow. Kyle started to bang his head—slightly at first, then so severely his parents thought sure he'd crack his skull wide open. Everything was in an uproar; nothing was going right.

Finally, one evening in the autumn of 1998, when Danita could take it no longer, she shut herself away in the garage, sat on the floor, and cried uncontrollably. She shouted at God, "Why are you doing this to my family? Why won't you help us?" Danita put her head in her lap and made a resignation. If help didn't come soon, she would end her life. She could not go on this way any longer.

In that one horrific moment, the tide began to turn. God heard Danita's cries. God was compassionate.

Immediately afterward, her mother invited Danita for a visit to California. She would leave Spokane and take a break from Kyle. She would get some much needed rest.

Then the first miracle happened. While at her mom's house, Danita read an article about a local newscaster in the morning paper. Her son had also been diagnosed with autism. Danita related to each one of the woman's struggles. She longed to have someone understand what she was going through. Without a moment's hesitation, Danita called the news station. She explained to a receptionist why she'd called, and the next thing Danita knew, only moments before airtime, the newscaster was on the phone, chatting with her as if they were old friends, offering compassion, offering advice, and most of all, offering help.

"You must get your son to California," the newscaster said. "As soon as you do, call me back, and I'll help you find the right connections, the best doctors, the right schools. I know it's hard, Danita, but I'm here. I'll do everything I can to help."

Danita returned home and begged her husband to move. He felt strongly that they should remain where they were—the schools, the doctors were all basically the same. They would find help for Kyle in Spokane. Danita shared her notebooks with him, notebooks filled with conversations, pleadings, and harsh rejections. Finally, Danita gave the situation over to God. If the Lord wanted them in California, He would have to open the door Himself. He would have to change her husband's heart.

Then the second miracle occurred. One day, without warning or explanation, Kyle's daddy looked into his son's eyes and realized that everything Danita had said was true. They would have to go, have to move away: this was Kyle's only hope. They packed their things and moved in faith toward God's open door.

Once they settled into their new apartment, Danita signed Kyle up for school. With much anticipation she brought him to his classroom to met the teacher—his "angel," as she now refers to him. He was an enthusiastic man with vast experience teaching autistic children. He promised Danita he'd take care of Kyle. Everything would improve. She would see; things were going to get better.

Kyle's teacher taught with a "communication board." If the students wanted something, they'd point to a picture. If they didn't have words, they would learn different ways to interact, to express their needs. For Kyle, this method of teaching was a new beginning. Soon he mastered it.

Then the third miracle occurred. One afternoon, Kyle arrived home from school. Danita was sitting beside him; his daddy was sitting on the arm of the couch. Kyle took his communication board, lifted the picture for *soda*, and pointed to it. Then, he spoke: "I want soda." Danita began to cry; his father literally fell off the couch. Their son could speak!

Kyle has continued to bloom with the help of many whom God sent across his path: a compassionate newscaster, parents who would give anything for their son, and an inspired, gifted teacher.

And now, the fourth miracle. Recently, Kyle amazed experts at an examination in San Francisco. The specialist hopes to see him in a regular kindergarten program next year. The doctor has never seen an autistic child so quickly come so far.

The fifth miracle and more? Well, they continue to unfold. His future is in God's hands now. And, for Kyle, God has only good things in store.

A Happy Meal

We've all seen the signs: "Will work for food." The first time I saw one, in the late 1980s on a busy California highway, I quickly pulled over and brought my car to a screeching halt. I nervously offered what I could, only to be lectured later by those more streetwise who had seen the signs numerous times before. For many, the pleas were not sincere offers to work, to labor hard in exchange for cash or a hot meal, but merely scams to play upon the guilt of others.

After that day, I wised up. I joined others with a quick judgment and a slight shake of the head. I was not going to be taken advantage of anymore.

But this time, only a few years later, the sign bearers were a family. A couple stood, clothes tattered, faces dirty, waiting with their two young children. Boy, that was really reaching! Even if it were a scam, how could I not give a meal to small, innocent children? I stopped, fumed a bit, and asked them what exactly was going on. The father explained in detail: the parents were out of work, out of money, could I possibly help?

In a hurry, and with only a few dollars in my purse—intended for a quick trip to the local coffee shop for my favorite luxury, a large, extra-rich mocha and a delicious almond croissant—I hesitated. If I bought them lunch, I couldn't indulge myself in my treat, in something I'd been looking forward to all afternoon.

Reluctantly, I mentally kissed my treat good-bye and agreed. With a smile and a promise, I asked the family to wait outside on the lawn. I walked through the parking lot, into the shopping center, and down several aisles. I stopped directly in front of the fast food counter. I ordered burgers for the parents, special meals for the kids, and sodas all around.

After the meals were ready and I provided the necessary cash, the clerk began to make change. To my surprise, he handed me several dollars too much. I pointed this out and then he stumped me: "You had to wait longer than expected because we had a mix-up in your order. We gave you a discount." Had I waited long? It didn't seem that I had. What kind of mix-up? I offered the money once more, but the clerk insisted.

I walked out of that burger place with cash still in my purse. The clerk had never known for whom the meals were intended. He couldn't have known; he couldn't have seen. But God had.

I happily delivered the meals to the famished parents and two smiling young children. Pleased, I wished them a good day. Then, with a song renewed in my heart, I drove to my favorite coffee shop and enjoyed God's simple rewards: a large, extra-rich mocha and a delicious almond croissant.

The Visitation

War—harsh, difficult times, moments filled with fear. Will loved ones return safely? When will the battles come to an end? Families alarmed by each phone call that might bring grave news.

For Mary, her faith in God helped to see her through. Both her son, Roy, and her younger brother, Larry, were fighting in the Korean War. Mary was worried for their safety, but she entrusted them both into God's gentle care. Each day, without fail, Mary would pray for God's protection, pray for guardian angels to surround them. And she believed.

No one wants to be caught off guard; it can make bad news harder, more difficult to accept. God understood that and sent Mary a message of preparation.

One early morning, after prayer, Mary had a remarkable vision. An angel, glowing in presence, beautiful in majesty, stood before her. Slowly, he began to speak. Roy and Larry had been wounded in action. They'd both been shot. Seeing the panic on Mary's face, the angelic being gently reassured her. Mary was not to worry, her brother and son would be all right. Then, as quickly as he arrived, the angel disappeared, leaving Mary amazed and shaken. "Shot—both of them! How could this be?" But the angel's words began to sink in, and Mary heeded the full message. They were shot, yes, but she was not to worry; they would be all right. She understood that God's angel had been sent to prepare her for bad news, to prepare her and yet offer comfort. Roy and Larry would be all right. That was all that mattered.

Mary began to thank God, thank Him for the warning, thank Him for the preparation, and thank Him for the promised, positive outcome. Her loved ones would survive. She would wait for the call.

She waited indeed, and then, just as she expected, the call arrived. The government had bad news. They were sorry to inform her that there had been an incident. Both her brother and son had been caught by enemy gunfire. They had been shot. As the officer spoke, the peace of God engulfed her.

Shortly after, when the men returned home, recovering from their wounds, her entire family celebrated with joy. Then she sat them all down next to a bright, roaring fire and told them, one by one, about her visitation, a visitation from an angel. And they were all amazed.

It's Darkest Before the Dawn

Everybody has one: a loved one who stubbornly refuses to see a doctor, even when it's obviously necessary to do so. Sometimes they're afraid, in denial—it will go away if ignored long enough. Sometimes they have a deep phobia—a fear of shots, tests, and extensive medical intervention. In Laura Taylor's family, this person was her mother, Carol.

Carol always took precautions with her children. Growing up, they never missed a checkup, and they had the best medical care in times of need. Yet for herself, ignorance was bliss. What she didn't know was wrong, was one less thing to worry about. That's just the way Carol was; there was no convincing her otherwise.

Throughout the 1970s, Carol had a growth on her leg. It was about the size of a silver dollar, hard as a rock, and each time Laura looked at it, fear struck her heart. Carol had never been to the doctor for a diagnosis, and one thing was clear: she was never going to do so. "It's nothing," she'd assure her daughter. But Laura was not convinced.

In 1979, Laura's worries increased. What if it were cancer? What if, by ignoring it, her mother died? Frustrated, Laura prayed. She asked God to heal her mom. Perhaps it was just a harmless cyst, but Laura couldn't be sure.

After three days, Laura's father had news. "Laura," he asked, "have you looked at your mother's leg? The growth looks much worse—it's turning colors, becoming soft. I'm very worried."

"Great," she thought. "Just when I begin to pray, the situation gets worse. Mom's had this growth for years, without any changes at all. Now what in the world is going on?"

Laura asked God for peace. The next morning, her mom informed her that the cyst had dissolved. After all of those years, just like that, it was gone forever.

God has continued to use this lesson in Laura's life. In the spiritual world, what appears to be is not always what is. Carol's cyst may have seemed to worsen, yet God was simply working on it, changing its form, so the healing could take place. What appeared, after prayer, to go downhill, was actually getting better. God could be trusted; He knew what He was doing.

Since that time, Laura's discovered that our human vision is limited, our understanding short-sighted. She's come to realize that God's answers are perfect, if we only have the faith to trust, to wait, to see.

A Place to Call Home

Cindy Huggins needed a place to call home, a place where she could rest and kick up her feet, a place that belonged just to her. For many years, she longed to have a home of her own. She had searched for an opportunity, but things never worked out as she planned. So Cindy continued to rent, to wait, and to pray.

In 1994, on a rainy afternoon, she received an eviction letter from her landlord. Her family had to move out. Devastated, Cindy prayed even harder. Where would they go? Would God provide a new place for them? Fear crushed her heart.

As her family began to pack, boxes stacking high, Cindy went into denial. She couldn't bring herself to help. She was afraid to go forward. Her husband, Tate, and three teenage children tried to encourage her. "We'll be fine. God will give us another place." But Cindy wasn't so sure. What if they were homeless—left out on the street? What if they had nowhere to go at all? She was terrified.

Within hours of the inevitable move, Cindy, brokenhearted, rested in her room. Just as she had feared, they had nowhere to go. "Lord," she prayed, "it's out of my hands. I give up." Exhausted, Cindy cried herself to sleep. While she slumbered, she had a dream. In her dream, she saw an outstretched hand. Then a soothing voice assured her: "Remember, you asked for this. Have faith."

With that, Cindy awoke. Yes, she had prayed to move, but certainly not like this. Her family had nowhere to go. But she began to hope, began to have faith. She got up and, for the first time, began to help pack.

It was late, and for a while, they drove aimlessly around town. Passing a friend's apartment building, Cindy suggested they stop for a visit. When they explained their predicament, the friend went to his landlord. There was the perfect apartment in his building, and it was vacant, cleaned, freshly painted, and ready for occupancy—their occupancy. Deposits were waived, and Cindy and her family happily moved in.

But God was not finished yet. Within a month, Cindy found a beautiful home for sale. She fell in love with it, and her heart, once again, began to hope. Could this be the house? Would God fulfill her desire now? She checked with the realtor. Everything looked perfect—except for one huge problem. Cindy was short on cash, $3,000 to be exact. Is this all that would stand in her way of a home, keep her from her dream once again?

Cindy went to work, but her mind was distracted. She could not concentrate. She ran the numbers through her head over and over again. Each time, she arrived at the same conclusion: they were still $3,000 short. Nothing could change that. Or could it?

Just then, her supervisor approached her. "What's the matter?" he asked.

Cindy shared her problem, her discouragement, with him. Then this man did a remarkable thing. Without hesitation, he went into his office and reemerged with his personal checkbook. He wrote out the draft, in Cindy's name, for the full amount needed: $3,000.

"You can't do this!" she insisted. "How will I ever pay you back?"

But her kind beneficiary simply smiled and said, "Cindy, I don't want you to return the money. It is a gift. If you paid me back, would I be rich? If you never paid me, would I be poor?" With that, he placed the check firmly in her hand and congratulated her on a dream accomplished. She was about to become a homeowner.

Cindy and her family still live in that beautiful house. She is grateful to the man who helped make her dream come true. Most of all, she is thankful to God—for answering her prayer, for moving a frightened young woman from security into the uncertain future. God had given Cindy the desire of her heart—a home to call her own.

Pushed in the Right Direction

C hange is never easy. Sometimes I get riveted to my position and hold on tightly, fearful of anything new. Often this occurs even when the status quo is not pleasant. Circumstances may not be perfect, but they are what I know, what I'm accustomed to.

In the autumn of 1986, I was pregnant with my first child. One late evening, out of the blue, my husband, Patrick, received a devastating call from his employer. He had discovered that Patrick had applied for other work. He was no longer welcome there. Once Patrick got over the shock, he took me aside and broke the news. He was out of a job.

To make matters worse, the next morning, after applying for unemployment, we discovered that his employer had not paid into the system at all. He had deducted the money from my husband's paychecks for years and then pocketed it himself. "It was fraud," the clerk informed us. We were simply out of luck.

Fortunately, within a few days, one of the applications came through with an offer. A great job—Patrick could start right away. There was only one condition: we must relocate from Sacramento to Redwood City, a town more than two hours away. Great job or not, I would hear nothing of it.

I'd lived in the same area all my life. I had many dear friends, my parents lived nearby, and I was pregnant with my first child. I absolutely refused to go. That was it; there was no changing my mind. I would pray for another solution. God would see it my way.

But He did not. A week went by with no prospects in sight. Patrick gently explained that while he knew it was hard for me, there was no option. He had a wife and a baby on the way. He had to work. It would only be a two-hour drive from home. We would come back often. Soon I'd like it, Patrick tried to assure me. But I was not convinced.

While I senselessly waited for a last-minute, pull-the-rabbit-out-of-a-hat kind of miracle, we packed our belongings and moved away from all I held so dearly.

I'd love to say I adjusted well. It would make me sound mature, but it's simply not true. I complained at every opportunity, compared the two cities (the new one always lost), and tolerated things at best.

In all fairness, I must admit that there were some wonderful times. Together with our young daughter, Tiffany, we visited fantastic places, and just as my husband had promised, we made frequent trips back home.

In less than a year, Patrick's new boss called him into his office. He had good news: there was a job opening in our hometown. We could relocate back to our roots. Did we still want to go? Did we? Of course we did! Within a month we had moved back to Sacramento.

It took time and distance to appreciate the full miracle. If Patrick had not lost his job, we would never have been so blessed. Although his new employer offered a much needed company car and more than double the pay, I would have convinced my husband not to accept the position if he had still held his original post. Because Patrick was laid off before the offer came in, God pushed us in the right direction, pushed us right into a blessing—one that, if left up to me, we would have missed altogether.

A Truck for Jeremy

A first vehicle—the pride and joy of a young man's heart. Becky Mitchell's son, Jeremy, was ready. He had saved his money wisely, and now Jeremy had a dream truck in mind. He searched the paper daily until one day he found it: the truck that fit his description perfectly.

Jeremy called the number, spoke to the owner, and then made an appointment to go see it. When mother and son arrived and he saw the truck, Jeremy could hardly contain his excitement. Every detail was exactly what he wanted—the color, the make, the year. The mileage was a little high, but the price was in his range. He had to have it. Becky smiled and nodded in agreement. Jeremy shook hands with the owner and promised to return shortly with a cashier's check—payment in full. The deal had been made. Becky's son was ecstatic!

Just a few minutes later, Jeremy returned with check in hand. But where was the truck? The man apologized and then told him what had happened. Just as they left, someone else had come to see the vehicle. He had offered more money, and the man had accepted. He was sorry, but the truck had been sold to another.

Jeremy was devastated. How could this be? Hadn't they made a deal? Wasn't his word, his handshake, good enough? Defeated, Jeremy drove home, not in a shiny new truck, but in his mother's car. On the drive home, Becky tried to convince him that things would work out for the best. What this man had done was wrong, unfair, but God had a better plan. If Jeremy would just have faith, then he would see. Her son, unconvinced, walked quietly into the house.

Becky was heartbroken for her son. She asked the Lord to comfort Jeremy. Oh, Becky knew that this was not a real crisis, an earth-shattering situation, but she wanted her son's faith restored, wanted him to see that God had his best interest at heart. She prayed for a blessing, and then she waited for God to answer.

Within a few days, on an afternoon drive with her husband, Becky came across a truck for sale. It was just like the one Jeremy so desperately wanted. However, this truck had low mileage and an even better price. Excited, she called him. She told Jeremy that this vehicle was perfect, an answer to prayer. Her son was not convinced. He didn't want to be disappointed again. Becky asked Jeremy if he could trust her to make the decision. Could she buy the truck and bring it home? Reluctantly, he agreed, and Becky did just that.

Later, as she pulled into the driveway, her son took one look at the beautiful, shiny truck and a smile began to break out all over his face. This was it—everything the other vehicle had been and more!

Jeremy learned many lessons that day—about the faith of his mother, about the goodness of God, about things really working out for the best. To this day, each weekend, Jeremy washes and waxes his truck until it shines. Then he drives through town proudly, waves to his friends, and offers them a quick smile.

Angels on the Highway

C arlos was a beautiful child, a bright, sweet, 18-month-old
boy. When Marta Marquez looked at her son, her eyes lit
up with the recognition of a mother who knew all children
were gifts from God. Marta loved Carlos and his two older
brothers with all her heart. She would have done anything to protect them, bless them, and watch over them with care. But Marta
knew that moms can't be everywhere. Her heartfelt prayer was
that God would send guardian angels to watch over her innocent
young babes.

One sunny afternoon in 1981, while her husband took the two
older boys on a fishing trip, Marta put little Carlos down for a nap.
This was a rare opportunity for a young mom, a chance for quiet,
for solitude, for some time to reflect.

Marta grabbed her Bible and headed for her bedroom. While
deep in prayer, she felt a strong tug at her spirit: "Get up and
check on Carlos!" Marta didn't hesitate or argue. She knew that
the gift of a mother's intuition is often the very voice of God. She
jumped to her feet, ran quickly to her baby's room, looked in his
bed, and was only slightly disturbed to find him not there.

"No reason to panic. I only put him down for a nap a few
moments ago. He must be down the hall playing," Marta assured
herself. But after a thorough search of the house, while she called
his name repeatedly, Marta could not find him. She ran for the
door, looked in the backyard, looked in the front. Then she quickly
reentered the house and ran room by room in search of her son.
Only this time her movements were more rapid, more frantic, and
her cries for her son more desperate and determined.

As she prayed for God's help, His wisdom, His intervention,
Marta got an idea. She ran for the backyard once again, but this
time she approached the fence. Sure enough, right before her eyes

was a broken board, large enough for a small child to squeeze through. "Please God, not there, not on that busy highway behind our home. Carlos can't be on that road!"

Then Marta heard their voices, their words, a distinct answer to her prayer: "Is this your little boy?"

Marta looked up, and there, sheltered by a middle-aged couple, was Carlos. The woman told Marta that they had spotted the toddler just as he came through the fence and began his journey across the highway. Grateful beyond words, and with the weight of fear lifted from her soul, Marta grabbed her young son, held him close, and thanked the couple for saving her boy's life.

As mother and son began the quick trip down the hill into the refuge of their home, Marta turned around to thank the couple once more. But, just like the guardian angels she had prayed for, they were gone: nowhere to be seen, nowhere to be found. They had accomplished their mission, appeared for a short time as an answer to prayer, and then continued on their way. Marta believes her son's guardian angels are traveling that highway still, perhaps in search of other moms whose hearts are filled with prayer.

A Marriage Made in Heaven

Many people search far and wide for a mate: someone to love, someone to care beyond measure. Countless individuals are never so fortunate to discover this joy in their lifetime. Judy Jenness has been blessed twice.

It was the 1960s. Judy was happily married with three wonderful children. Suddenly, when she was only 26, she lost her husband—widowed at such a young age. Friends and family tried to console her, but Judy knew her hope was in God. No one else could understand the sorrows of her soul. God heard Judy's cries as she'd duck into a room, away from her children, to let it all out. She had to be strong for her kids, strong for everyone, but God knew the truth.

After a while, when healing took place, she started to wonder. Would she ever love again? Would anyone want a woman with three young children? Was there any man who would love them as his own? Judy knew it was a tall order, but she began to pray. And God was listening.

Soon afterward, while having dinner at a local cafe, she glanced across the table. There sat a stranger, a gorgeous man, and his smile caught hers. They began to chat. He was new in town, transferred from San Francisco. Judy, being the friendly sort, introduced herself to Mac, and they struck up a friendship.

Over the next two weeks, Judy took him around town, showed Mac the sights, served him home-cooked meals, and introduced him to her kids. Mac didn't run away; he stayed right by the side of this beautiful widow and her ready-made family.

As quickly as the whirlwind romance began, he asked the question. Would she be his wife? Judy agreed, and with the blessings of her children, they were married—an answer to prayer, a dream come true.

They grew in faith, a family bonded together by love. Mac soon adopted all of Judy's children—all of "their" children. Then soon there was more to celebrate. A baby was on the way! They prepared for the birth with excitement. Their daughter Devonne came into this world, making them a complete family of six.

Judy and Mac have been married for more than 34 years now. They are still blissful, still thankful, and still believe in the miracle of love.

Judy knows that God answers prayers. For she has been blessed so much. She's had the good fortune of a second chance at life—a second chance at love. Who could ask for more?

A Christmas to Remember

For Lauri Enloe and her family, the early 1990s were difficult times: a young married couple, an out-of-work husband, three small children, and Christmas just days away. Lauri wasn't sure how it would all work out, but work out, she knew it must. These were just children, her children, and she couldn't deny them Christmas.

Things had never been easy, marrying so young, three babies arriving soon after, but they'd always made it; they'd always survived. This time, things were not that simple—a husband laid off from work and no money coming in at all. Lauri didn't know where to turn. She thought back to her own youth, each Christmas of the past. Then she thought of her childhood faith, and she began to pray: "Please, God, not for myself, not for my husband, but for our children. Please don't let Christmas pass them by."

Lauri didn't let circumstances get her down. She was determined to have Christmas whether there were gifts or not. Her children would celebrate; they would celebrate together. She read the story of Christ's birth. They sang carols at bedtime. Together they roasted marshmallows and drank spiced cider. Christmas would not pass them by.

Then, on Christmas Eve, there was a knock at their door. A stranger, dressed not in a festive red suit but in dark military fatigues, handed them presents. As mysteriously as he arrived, he left again, into the cold, foggy night air.

As they snuggled together by the fire, the children squealed with excitement. Lauri allowed each child to open one gift. They tore open the presents, wildly giggling with anticipation. Out of the boxes emerged three pairs of beautiful red pajamas with matching satin slippers. The children ran to put them on, and to Lauri's surprise, everything fit perfectly.

The next morning, as the sun barely had time to rise, the little ones woke their parents. It was time to open the rest of the gifts; it was time to celebrate Christmas! Lauri and her husband got up, and one by one, the children opened their presents. They each received an outfit and a new toy to call their own.

Lauri never discovered who their kind benefactor was. But she knows one thing for sure: he was like an angel, sent as an answer to prayer. He brought the fulfillment of a mother's wish for her children, a wish that Christmas would not pass them by.

Ever since that night, Christmas comes to the Enloe home just on time, without a hitch. But the true, giving spirit of the season joyfully remains in their hearts all year through.

A Friendship Like No Other

In our lives, many people come and go. But to have one true friend, one close bond in a lifetime, that is a gift. Oh, there are acquaintances and casual relationships; there are friendships that can last for years. But rare is the person who experiences such closeness; the angels themselves stand up and take notice.

Sharon Schoenfeld had such a relationship with her dear friend John. They'd known each other since the 1970s. While they were attending a Napa Valley high school, they shared secrets of the heart, laughter, and sorrow. Many times they'd sit over mugs of steaming hot coffee, talking for hours, dreaming of their futures. They studied together, cheered from the crowd at local football games, and shared many quiet picnic lunches. There was never a romance, for they were interested in others. Yet there was a bond nonetheless, an unquestionable sense of commitment they both knew was sent from above.

By 1984, Sharon had married and John was engaged. He had celebrated at her wedding, and she looked forward to celebrating at his. A church was arranged for the ceremony, and his best man and ushers were chosen. The marriage would soon take place.

Then Sharon had a dream. She dreamt she was in church; John's family was all around. Their friends were there, but this was not a wedding. People were crying. What was going on? Then Sharon saw John's brother, embraced by his father. They sobbed uncontrollably. What was the matter? Bob was a missionary overseas; why was he in California? As suddenly as the dream began, it ended. Sharon woke up, startled, confused, and crying. What had the dream meant? Was it a warning of things to come or just a meaningless nightmare? Sharon had no answers.

Shortly thereafter, John made a business call to her husband. They talked for a while. When they finished, John said, "Be sure to tell Sharon 'good-bye.'"

In the middle of the night, they got the call. John had died suddenly; a fatal asthma attack had struck only seconds after he'd hung up the phone. He was only 26.

A few days later, at his funeral, Sharon sat in the church, the very church he had reserved for his wedding. His best man and ushers were assigned the solemn duty of carrying John's casket. Sharon was surrounded by friends. They were all crying. She looked to her left and saw John's brother Bob, returned from the mission field, embracing his father. They sobbed uncontrollably. Then Sharon remembered her dream.

Many years have passed, and Sharon still thanks God for the special bond between them. She knows that such a deep and sacred friendship is a gift from heaven, for it has no other source. From their closeness came a dream, ahead of schedule, preparing her for the loss to come. From their closeness came his final words: "Be sure to tell Sharon 'good-bye.'" Neither knowing the future, neither understanding what would be, but both influenced by a great and powerful love, a love that will last for eternity.

A Foolish Plan

The teen years can be difficult—trying new things, not having the discretion to make wise decisions. Sometimes we're so sure of ourselves, so headstrong, that if it were not for the grace of God, we'd surely fall.

In 1972, 16-year-old Maggie and her 13-year-old cousin, Leann, spent the night at their grandparents' comfortable Northern California home. The girls were excited at the prospect of seeing each other. Living several hours apart, they rarely had the opportunity to visit more than a few times a year. The two teenagers played cards, ate far too many potato chips, and performed exotic beauty makeovers.

As the evening wore on, the girls tired of their games and grew increasingly restless. While their grandparents slept, they schemed up a plan. Now, Maggie and Leann were basically good kids. They had never used drugs and did not drink alcohol. But on this particular night, the two cousins were bored, naive—and, as it turned out, dangerously foolish. They had heard that breathing the fumes of a certain kitchen product produced a slight high. They had heard it was harmless. They had heard it was fun. They had heard wrong!

Knowing that their grandmother always kept this product in her kitchen, the girls mischievously went to retrieve it. Not finding the item, they began to search further. Maggie and Leann took product after product out of the cupboard, placing each on the floor until they'd come to the end of the cabinet. It wasn't there; their grandmother must have been out of it. The girls dismissed the plan as foolish and went to bed.

Early in the morning, Maggie and Leann awakened to the sound of the radio alarm. The news was on, and these were the very first words they heard: "Two teens in San Francisco died last night breathing the fumes of a common kitchen product." The reporter went on to describe the very item the girls had searched for just the night before. The girls had no idea it was unhealthy, dangerous, even deadly. Thank God their grandparents had been out of the product. Maggie and Leann's lives had been spared!

Stunned and grateful, the girls could barely speak. Methodically, they dressed and stumbled into the kitchen for breakfast. Maggie and Leann decided to make their favorite breakfast— toast and sunny-side-up eggs. As Maggie opened the cupboard to grab the cooking oil, she suddenly froze with shock. There, right in front, in the very cabinet they'd searched the night before, was the deadly product.

Maggie and Leann believe that God, in His goodness, protected them with angelic blinders. He gave two foolish teens a chance, a warning, and most important, He saved their lives. Maggie and Leann will never understand why two teens died on the same night their lives were spared. But they will always be grateful for a second chance—a chance to learn, to grow wiser, and to serve God in the future. Maggie and Leann hope to serve Him well.

A Kind Deed Remembered

A young boy of seven, racing down the street, sirens blaring, excitement in the air. It was 1930, and little Jimmy Mulligan loved to go to work with his father. His dad didn't have just any boring job. No, his father was the local assistant fire chief. How Jimmy loved to go along, racing wildly through the long, narrow streets, pretending he was a fireman on his way to an emergency.

But one day the fun and games almost ended. The vehicle they rode in was suddenly broadsided. It flipped over, and young Jimmy was pinned underneath. Frantic, his father waved down the next passerby—a local mailman. The man ran as quickly as he could to help Jimmy's father lift the vehicle and free the young child. Jimmy was out, he was alive, but he was seriously injured. An artery in his wrist had been ruptured; he was bleeding profusely.

Together, father, son, and mailman rushed to the hospital. The benevolent mailman clutched Jimmy's seriously gashed wrist, keeping him from losing even more blood than he already had. This man helped to save little Jimmy's life.

When the last sutures were finished, and Jimmy was released to go home, the three cried, exchanged hugs, and then went on their way.

Many years came and went, and young Jimmy grew into a fine young man. Having a deep spiritual side and a compassion for others, he joined the priesthood. Father Mulligan served people far and wide and held in his heart a deep love for God.

When he served communion and caught a glimpse of his scar, he'd once again thank God for sparing his life. He'd say a silent prayer for his hero, wherever he might be.

One afternoon, Father Mulligan was walking the halls of his church. He heard a great commotion in the next room. What was going on? He decided to find out. A woman was crying uncontrollably. He asked her what was wrong. Then the story came spilling out. Her wedding was scheduled to take place in two days. Relatives and friends were coming from miles around. Every detail had been planned: the wedding dress hung in her closet, the food was being prepared as they spoke, the flowers were already ordered. Now, a dispensation error had created havoc—her wedding had suddenly been called off.

Father Mulligan calmed the young woman and quickly picked up the phone. After a few minutes, things looked brighter. He would take care of everything. The wedding would go on as planned.

As they exchanged hugs, the woman mentioned that she knew of a local family named Mulligan. More than 20 years ago, her father had saved their young boy's life. Were they possibly related? Father Mulligan leaned back for a moment, took it all in, and then, shaking, he began to speak. He was the young boy; it was his life her father had saved! Together they rejoiced—she for a wedding that would go on as planned, he for finding a long lost-friend.

Father Mulligan joyfully performed their wedding ceremony. At the reception, he had the honor of seeing the father of the bride—his hero. They hugged, they cried, and Father Mulligan once again thanked him for saving his life. A kind deed remembered, a kind deed returned, just the way little Jimmy Mulligan would have wanted it.

In Pursuit of a Miracle

Four friends, traveling across California in pursuit of a miracle. It was the mid-1970s. Judy Jenness, with friends Geneva, Virginia, and Geneva's teenage daughter, Cindy, set out on the road. They were on the way to a crusade, a crusade they hoped would bring healing for Virginia.

Virginia was suffering from multiple sclerosis. She was a dear friend, and the women were convinced that if they could get to the crusade—if they could get Virginia there soon enough—she would be healed. There was excitement in the air. They prayed, packed their belongings, threw them in the back of Judy's VW bus, and headed off to find a miracle. Everyone would surely be astonished when they returned home.

They journeyed for hours, laughed, sang songs, and prayed. They prayed for a safe trip, they prayed for a wonderful crusade, and they prayed for a miracle. When the women arrived, they pulled into the parking lot and then joined the long line of people waiting outside. Soon they made their way into the building. They had finally made it! The auditorium was electric with anticipation.

First there was time set aside for worship. The women sang along, in awe of God's presence, thankful for the opportunity just to be there. Then the minister began to speak—his words so eloquent, his soul so alive. They soaked up each word. They knew that any second they'd receive what they came for; they'd receive a miracle.

Between sacred moments, there were times of joy. At one point, when the minister compared the temperament of some people to that of donkeys, Geneva, overexcited, rose her hand high. The other women giggled so much, they thought they'd be escorted outside.

Finally, it was time—the moment had arrived. The call had been made to pray for the sick. Virginia, along with many others, rose to her feet. There was no doubt about it, God heard each and every prayer. Some were healed instantly. Some would be healed later. Yet some were not healed at all, but simply left wondering. Virginia was one of the latter.

With the crusade over, the four women walked back to the van, a little less energetic, a lot more quiet. Why had Virginia not been healed? They had believed so much, been so sure God would comply.

For the most part, the drive home was solemn, except for a brief round of giggles. The sun had been blazing. Due to the intense heat, each of them took one of Virginia's water pills. The medicine worked well. There was only one problem: there was no bathroom in sight. The only thing close was an empty coffee can. You can guess just how they put it to use. The women, once again, got the giggles, water retention and all, over coffee cans and donkeys, over special moments among friends.

It has been many years since the four went on their journey in pursuit of a miracle. Since then, Geneva has passed on, and Virginia still has multiple sclerosis. But the women learned something that day. Sometimes, God doesn't answer prayer just the way we'd like. But He taught them about friendship, about being there for each other, about sticking together through thick and thin. Virginia was their companion, and they'd stand by her, help her as long as they were able. That was all God asked. That was all He required.

A journey—traveling in an old VW bus in pursuit of a miracle. It just so happens they found one after all. The four women discovered the miracle of friendship, one that will bind them together for all eternity.

The Breakthrough

Teachers and students—sometimes their relationship can be more than academic. Sometimes they offer friendship and wisdom; sometimes they can even help to mend a broken heart. In 1988, Sharon Schoenfeld had such a friendship with a seven-year-old student named Paul.

Paul was in her special education class. He had many problems, both emotional and neurological. To add to his troubles, his home life was rough. His parents were on and off drugs; Paul was a child caught in the middle, trying to understand.

Paul didn't trust anyone, he made that quite clear. Sharon tried to reach out to him with compassion. Paul, not being used to kindness, wasn't sure what to make of her.

Frustrated, Sharon began to pray. Each night, before she fell asleep, she asked God for a way to break through, even if only for a moment, to convince Paul she truly cared. Then she'd smile with assurance and say, "Amen."

Soon afterwards, Paul approached his teacher. "My hand hurts," he whimpered. Sharon lifted his Band-Aid, and upon inspection saw just what was wrong: a piece of barbed wire embedded in his hand, left unattended to fester. Sharon went to the phone and called his mother. She explained that Paul must be taken to the doctor immediately; this injury could not remain untreated. Then Sharon got a taste of the difficult life Paul led.

His mother, speech slurred from drugs, told her son's teacher how the injury had occurred. Paul had been late for dinner. He was too busy climbing fences to come in. The barbed wire—well, it was simply God's way of "punishing" him for being late.

Before Paul left for the doctor, Sharon sat him down. She told Paul she was sorry about his injury. She told him she cared. Then she broke school rules just a bit when she added, "And God cares about you, too."

Paul gazed at her, confusion in his eyes—a little hope, a little skepticism. Could anyone really care for him? Could God?

The next morning he returned to class, his hand much improved. He sat quietly at his desk and with great detail began to draw. When he finished, he smiled proudly, folded his masterpiece into sections, and brought it to her desk. When Sharon unfolded his gift, she discovered a sketch of brightly colored flowers. Then Paul began to speak: "I don't have money to buy real flowers, so I drew them for you instead. Thanks for caring about me."

The next year Paul changed classes. With a new room and a new teacher, it was time to go their separate ways. Paul was scared. He told Sharon he'd miss her, that she was the only one in his life who ever truly cared.

Over the years, Sharon's lost touch with Paul. To this day, she wonders how he is. Every night before she falls asleep, Sharon still prays for Paul. She asks God to comfort him, to show Paul he's loved, to remind him she still cares. Sharon rests in the assurance that no matter what Paul had been told, God loves Paul, too. It was God's very compassion that brought them together, even if only for a season. She thanks God for a folded-up drawing, flowers just for her, revealing, if only for a moment, that she finally broke through. Then she smiles with assurance and says, "Amen."

A Timely Answer

They had dated for more than a year. Meghan and Mark were in love. Mark was sensitive, kind, loving—everything Meghan had dreamed of. He was her ideal mate, except for one thing: Mark had a drinking problem.

They shared their hopes and dreams. They spoke of marriage. But nothing definite was planned. Mark's drinking concerned Meghan, concerned her enough to put off the decision.

It was August 1985, the weather was hot, and Meghan left California for New York—a vacation to see her father. While there, Mark weighed heavily upon her mind. As Meghan climbed into bed, she prayed. She asked God to watch over him, to help him stop drinking, to keep Mark from the dangerous path he was on. Meghan decided that, even if they were not meant to be together, even if they never married, she still wanted Mark well. She cared for him that much. A quiet peace fell over her. Somehow, she knew that everything would be all right. She fell asleep in the assurance that God had answered her prayer.

When Meghan returned to California, Mark paid her a visit. When he set his backpack on the floor, a piece of paper fell out. It was a ticket—a ticket for a D.U.I. Then he explained. He'd been driving under the influence; he'd been pulled over by an officer. In all his years of drinking, this had never happened before. He told Meghan that the ticket was a good thing. It had brought him to a realization that his drinking was out of control. He had made a vow that night, a promise that he'd never take a sip of alcohol again.

Meghan and Mark married that year. Their marriage is blessed with happiness. Together, they have a good life: a lovely California home and three beautiful daughters. Meghan knows

God answers prayer: the ticket was dated August 20, 7:00 P.M. (10:00 P.M. E.S.T.)—the exact moment she'd prayed. It's been nearly 15 years now, and by the grace of God, Mark has been good to his promise; he's never taken another drink. And God watches over him still.

A Granddaughter's Story

There's a special connection between children and their grandparents, a sacred bond that reaches deep into their souls. Building that relationship meant everything to Angie Willey. She desired that her daughter, Chela, would treasure her grandparents always.

Angie Willey got her wish. Chela loved visiting her grandparents' home. They showered her with hugs, kisses, and the attention that every young child deserves. They baked her cookies, read her stories, and took her for strolls on sunny afternoons.

But, as life sometimes will have it, their time together was cut short. In the early 1990s, Angie's father-in-law developed cancer, and after a few months of struggle, he passed away.

Chela missed her grandpa, but in time she began to mention him less. Angie was concerned. Would Chela quickly forget him? She was so young when he died, not quite two years old. All her hopes for lifelong memories seemed doomed to end. That is, until Angie prayed, "Please God, keep Chela's heart open to Grandpa's memory; never allow their special tie to be broken."

A few months later, Chela sat at the kitchen table. With soft brown hair cascading over her shoulders, she intently began to draw. An artist at work, she quietly sang the "Happy Birthday" song. When Chela was finished, she presented her mother with a picture. "It's a birthday card for Grandpa," she proudly announced. With a quick smile, her mom promised to deliver it to Grandma for safekeeping.

Later that afternoon, they drove to Grandma's home. Angie wanted to pay her a visit, to check in and see how Grandma was doing. Ever since Grandpa had died, Chela's visits brought her a special sort of cheer. When Chela gave Grandma the card, the dear woman gasped at the sight. "How did you know it was Grandpa's birthday today?"

"I'm not sure. I just know," Chela replied with childlike innocence.

Angie was confused. She had no idea it was really her father-in-law's birthday. How could Chela have known? Angie quickly called her husband at work. Had he told Chela of the occasion? No, he had forgotten himself. He had not mentioned a thing.

As Chela brushed her light brown hair out of her face, she smiled intently at her grandmother.

Suddenly, everything seemed to stand still, and Angie finally understood. Chela had no earthly way of knowing, but she had a heavenly one. Chela knew because God in his faithfulness had answered Angie's prayers. Chela's special bond with her grandpa had transcended time, even transcended death. It's a sacred gift she treasures still.

Miracle in Monaco

Yvonne and Gordon Scholz had been traveling for days on a much anticipated European vacation, visiting relatives and seeing the sights. On this particular afternoon, they drove the streets of Monaco, enjoying every twist and turn, every moment of their trip. The small country was beautiful, just like they'd seen in the pictures. It was everything they'd dreamed of.

While visiting Monaco, Yvonne wanted to visit the grave of Princess Grace. She desired to bring flowers, say a prayer, and give honor to a woman she'd admired for so long. When they arrived, Yvonne bowed her head and offered a prayer. She prayed for Princess Grace and the children she'd left behind. She prayed for Monaco: for its people and their needs. Then Yvonne lifted her head, turned quietly, and headed back for the car.

As she walked, Yvonne realized how little time she regularly spent in prayer. In her day-to-day activities, she was so busy she rarely stopped and spoke to God about her needs. She vowed, in that moment, to do it more often.

As Yvonne approached the car, she noticed they'd done the unthinkable. While in a rush, they'd carelessly locked their keys inside the vehicle. Try as they might, they could not open the door.

Here they were, stuck in a foreign country, not knowing the language, and with keys locked inside their car. How would they get safely back to their hotel? Just as she began to panic, Yvonne decided to heed her vow. She would take a moment, say a prayer, then wait for God's reply. Before she knew it, the answer was on its way.

Suddenly, a man about to whiz by the highway saw their parked car and pulled over. "Do you need help?" he asked.

They tried to explain their trouble. Somehow, between the man's broken English and their limited French, they were able to communicate. He understood their dilemma. He was a locksmith. He could be of help. "A locksmith traveling the same highway and stopping just at the moment we need him. Surely, this is God's providence!" Yvonne rejoiced. The locksmith didn't want any money. He simply desired to assist the young couple. Within a few minutes, he opened the door and handed them the key. The relieved couple offered him a hug, thanked him, and soon, with a beep of the horn, were on their way.

Yvonne had a wonderful time in Monaco. She enjoyed the sights, and to this day, she treasures many precious memories. But mostly she treasures the lesson that remains with her still. Since that time, Yvonne takes a moment each day to say a quiet prayer. Then she calmly lifts her head and waits for God's reply.

Day Care Provider

When Lauri McCallum received notice that her day care worker was leaving her business, she began to panic. Who could she trust with her eighteen-month-old daughter, Elisabeth? What would she do?

Lauri thought and thought, but she couldn't come up with a solution. She only had a few days to find alternate care. Her job would not wait. Desperate, she cried out to God for help: "Please show me where to take my daughter. Please lead me to the right person who will nurture and care for her."

On her way to run errands, Lauri drove past a local church. Suddenly, she felt an impulse to go inside. Lauri wasn't sure why. Yes, she knew they provided day care, but her daughter was months below the two-year age requirement. Still, she felt drawn into the parking lot, out of her car, and inside the office. Casually, not knowing what else to say, she asked to see their program. While the director took her around, she wondered why she was there. Surely, this could not be her answer, not at least for several months. But what about now? She needed a solution today. Didn't God have a calendar?

Finally, unable to hold it in any longer, Lauri told the director everything. Words came pouring out, words of helplessness, words of desperation. Her daughter was too young for the program. Lauri needed an answer today. What could she do? The director smiled, thought for a moment, and then offered an answer. She might know of a person to provide child care. There was a wonderful woman—she adored children, was responsible, kind, and had taught at their school for years. She had recently opened a day care in her home. Would Lauri be interested in her number? Lauri smiled broadly and accepted the information with joy.

Calls were made, appointments followed. Yes, she had found a day care provider in just the nick of time. Not just any provider, but a wonderful woman, one who was everything Lauri had hoped and prayed for. It turns out God did have a calendar after all, and a little something more. He also had an active list of names and phone numbers, just the right information to answer a young mother's prayers.

The Eleventh Hour

*I*n 1985, when Karen and Tom were newlyweds, they decided to earn some extra cash. Tom's full-time job as a mechanic and Karen's part-time job as a teaching assistant were barely enough to make ends meet. The plan went like this: Tom would buy an old car, fix it up, and then sell it for a tidy profit. It sounded like a great idea to both of them. So within a few days, Tom found an old car—a beat-up Toyota—paid $400 and got to work. He worked on the engine, changed the seat covers, and polished the vehicle until it shined. Then Tom parked the car at the auto shop, put a "For Sale" sign in the window, and patiently waited.

A few days later, an acquaintance stopped by Tom's work for a quick visit. Within moments, the gentleman inquired about the Toyota. When Tom showed him the vehicle and took him for a test drive, the man quickly made the purchase.

"Sold for $800!" Tom excitedly told Karen when he returned home from work.

Everything went fine until a few months later, when a parking ticket arrived at their home. "Oh, no," Karen thought. "This man never changed the registration or signed a release of liability. How do we prove we're not to blame?" Then worse thoughts began to cross Karen's mind: "If he were in an accident, we could be held liable."

Karen hounded Tom constantly, asking him to find the buyer and straighten out the overlooked detail. But, try as he might, Tom was unable to locate him, and Karen began to fume.

Several weeks later, around 11:00 A.M., the car once again crossed her mind. Just as she began to fret, Karen realized how much she had taken the problem out on Tom. After all, it wasn't his fault. His intentions had been good. She made a mental note to apologize to her husband that night. Then Karen had a novel idea.

Why not take this problem to God? Surely, He understood how to solve it. God knew exactly where this man was. Karen asked God to find the buyer and release them from any liability. For the first time in months, Karen felt at peace.

That night, when Tom returned from work, he casually mentioned, "The man who bought our car came into the shop today." Thrilled, Karen asked if they'd taken care of the necessary paperwork. They had. Karen hesitated, for just a moment, and then asked, "When did he come in?"

"Eleven o'clock this morning," Tom replied.

God had been right on time.

A Doe and Her Fawn

Mistakes made, damage done, sometimes there's no turning back. Try as we might to correct the wrong, others often pay the price. Because of her past, Sue Renz feared for her sons' futures. Oh, she'd been a good mother throughout the 1970s, had always loved her three boys, but faith had not been a part of her children's early upbringing. When Sue was younger, she had even dabbled in the occult. But that was all behind her now. Sue had recognized the need for God in her life and had joyously embraced the Christian faith. But she worried incessantly for the lost years—her sons' early spiritual development. Sue wondered if it was too late to spare them a similar dark, spiritual journey.

In 1988, with her sons now 6, 12, and 13, Sue desperately prayed for their futures. She prayed for freedom from the cloak of darkness she had unknowingly rested upon their shoulders.

Soon afterwards, she was invited on a Christian retreat. Sue made her reservations, packed her bags and headed, as they say, straight for the hills. While on the retreat, Sue began reading a wonderful book. The writer addressed Sue's fears, addressing the damage we do to others, even to our own innocent children. And the book offered hope. God could break this chain of darkness and free anyone from its power.

After the retreat, she made a call to an acquaintance. As she began to share, Sue was invited for prayer. Together, they'd believe for God's forgiveness. They prayed for freedom from bondage, freedom from the effects of past wrongs on both her present and her future. They prayed that the chain would be broken and that her children would be set free. Several times the woman asked God to give Sue a sign, but nothing appeared to change.

When the time of prayer ended and Sue rose to leave, the two women embraced. Then Sue began the long drive home. As she pulled out onto the highway, she picked up speed. Suddenly, without warning, her headlights caught the glimpse of a mother doe and her baby fawn, standing in the middle of the road. Unable to stop quickly enough, Sue laid on her horn, hoping for their safety. The mother deer moved rapidly to the side, but the little fawn stood frozen in its tracks, caught by the mesmerizing glow from her illuminated headlights. A quick swerve, a moment in time, the mother deer barely to her left, the baby fawn inches to her right. Sue had missed them both! Doe and fawn were safe. As she thanked God for protecting them, she heard a still, small voice begin to speak within her: "Sue, this is your sign. As I care for a doe and her fawn, how much more do I care for you and your children."

Sue knows that the God of love has forgiven her and has freed her offspring from chains of darkness. He's lifted a mother and her children away from harm, like a doe and her fawn safe from the path of a speeding car.

The Messenger

Marcia and Stephanie are true friends. They grew up together, spending long afternoons practicing cartwheels on Marcia's front lawn. Their memories are filled with laughter, joy, and a few childhood arguments. They attended each other's weddings and were there for the birth of their children. Whether life's path is lined with roses or a journey filled with struggles, Marcia and Stephanie always walk together.

We live in a fast-paced, busy world. Sometimes we hardly have a moment for ourselves, let alone time to nurture old friendships. There are seasons when Marcia's and Stephanie's hectic schedules will separate them for months, but the two women have a clear understanding that they're both available in times of need. For Marcia and Stephanie, it only takes a moment to rekindle a lifetime of history.

In the summer of 1978, as the two women sat at a local cafe, drinking coffee and enjoying a scrumptious piece of chocolate pie, Marcia began to share the struggles in her life. She had just broken up with a long-time boyfriend and was searching for new direction, new meaning for her future. Soon it became apparent that Marcia's needs were about more than relationships and new directions; they were spiritual in nature. Stephanie suggested that her friend stop by a church to speak with a pastor. Perhaps this would help Marcia sort through her problems, clarify the situation, and grant her some peace about circumstances beyond her control. Marcia agreed to make an appointment with Stephanie's pastor, whom Stephanie was certain would gladly meet with her.

As the discussion continued, however, Marcia started to change her mind. As much as she wanted direction, she began to pull back—as we all sometimes do—to hesitate, to retreat. Maybe spiritual counseling wasn't what she needed after all. Maybe she'd wait. Things would work themselves out.

While Marcia and Stephanie finished their chocolate pie and began contemplating a second piece, a man walked through the parking lot, through the door of the cafe, and, without hesitation, approached their table. He seemed to ignore everyone else in the room. When he spoke, he looked directly into Marcia's misty green eyes: "I'm not sure why I'm here, but I feel I should invite you to my church." Then he went on to mention the house of worship he attended. It was the very place the two women had just been discussing. The man looked away, as if a little embarrassed for the intrusion, spun around on his heels, and quickly walked out of the building.

Initially Marcia thought Stephanie had put him up to it, but Stephanie was finally able to convince her friend that she'd never seen the man before in her life. It was a huge congregation. Stephanie did not know him. In fact, she never saw him again. But, his presence was just the extra encouragement Marcia needed. She did call for an appointment with the pastor, and she followed up with an afternoon of counseling. Situation taken care of—problem solved. A deeper spiritual connection, stronger faith, and renewed prayer life spun her into a positive direction.

To this day, Marcia and Stephanie stand by each other in times of need. But they understand that some problems are too large, some burdens too heavy, for even their strong shoulders to handle. It's then that they put their struggles into the hands of God, and He gently carries them through.

The Move

Angie Willey doesn't like change. She takes comfort in the status quo, a certain dependability in life that brings, for her, not boredom but a feeling of peace and tranquillity. Her home, cozy and tasteful, will surely remain decorated the same for years to come. She likes certain foods, never too adventurous; a specific style of clothing; and, most of all, good old dependable friends she can count on for a lifetime. That's the way Angie likes it, and for the most part, that's the way her life's played out.

That is, until a quiet afternoon in 1988, when her husband got word he'd received a promotion. A better job—good news; more money—definitely good news; a move several hundred miles away—wait a minute, not so fast! But, there was no way around it; the move was imminent. Angie resigned herself to make the best of the situation.

Now, she must admit, there was a certain element of excitement involved, a tiny hope for a new and brighter future. But what of her volunteer work at the local school? What of her church—a wonderful parish she'd so grown to love? What of the long afternoons with dear and loyal friends, talking, laughing, and drinking a soothing cup of tea?

In a matter of a few months, their home had been put on the market, sold, and another one purchased. The new community was nice. It definitely had its advantages, but it was not yet home. Her friends were so far away, e-mail and telephone calls became a daily necessity. Angie tried her best to make the move positive for her family. She got involved in her daughter's school, sewed curtains for the house, and she began to pray. She prayed for direction, for joy, and for new friends sure to come her way.

Then, a few weeks later, it happened. Angie went on a short walk to scope out the neighborhood. She passed a lady walking in the opposite direction. They briefly glanced up, smiled, and said, "Hello." As she walked by, the woman shouted, "Angie, is that you?" Angie spun around, and to her shock, she discovered it was her dear friend Dorothy. Dorothy was a pal from her old neighborhood. She had moved almost seven years earlier, and the two women had somehow lost touch. They could hardly believe it. Here they were, hundreds of miles from where they started, yet they ended up moving just a few short blocks apart. They laughed, they hugged, and then they went home and told their families.

Angie has long since settled into her new home, and, if you can keep a secret, she's decided she loves it. She's made many wonderful friends, and she still keeps in touch with the old. Angie is grateful that God gave her the comfort of an old pal to help pave the way to acceptance. She remembers to thank Him for His goodness each time she takes a stroll down the street or has Dorothy over for an afternoon chat, a good laugh, and a soothing cup of tea.

Every Last Detail

*I*t was a difficult time, filled with more challenges than she could have ever imagined. Joyce Merriam's husband was out of work on a medical disability. For several months, they'd need to make every dollar stretch. The couple had decided the illness was enough adjustment for their family without throwing their lives into more chaos. Joyce had always stayed home with their children. For now, things would remain the same.

Joyce clipped coupons, saved pennies, and got by as best she could. Each purchase, whether it was hamburger for dinner or a small toy for a birthday, was first prayed over. There was absolutely no room for frivolous spending. Joyce was a wise shopper and could sniff out a garage sale five miles away: a child's book for a dime, to be enjoyed later by the light of a roaring fire; a lamp for a quarter, to brighten an old room; soft, lacy curtains for 50 cents, just the kind her little girl had always wanted.

The home Joyce lived in was old, its kitchen dreary. There was no money in the budget for redecorating, but little by little, Joyce saved a dime here, a quarter there, and she began to pray. When she'd finally saved just enough for a gallon of paint, she went to the store and carefully chose the most beautiful, sunny yellow palette she could find. Not too bright, not too pale; it was perfect. How this color would lift her spirits. She imagined cooking eggs on a Sunday morning, toast popping up, children scrambling to their seats, and yellow walls almost singing, "Good Morning."

Joyce spent the afternoon painting. Little by little, stroke by stroke, the room began to take on an entirely new personality. She was thrilled. She was thrilled, that is, until her eyes gazed upon a large doorknob going from her kitchen to the outside patio. It was old, worn, dull brass. It was filled with scratches. She had never noticed it before, but now, with her sunny new walls, it seemed to jump right out and mock her every attempt at change. Now, with doorknob in full view, Joyce could no longer see the beautiful, sunny walls. To make matters worse, the lock was the old type with a skeleton key; she'd never find one like it. There was no money to replace it. She'd just have to make do.

Over the next few days, Joyce fought off the desire to be disappointed, to focus only on the negative. One Saturday morning, she asked God for forgiveness and began to thank Him for her many blessings. Then she did what she loved to do. Joyce drove off to enjoy an afternoon at a neighborhood garage sale.

The moment she arrived, her eyes saw it. It glistened in the sunlight; it shone brightly as if calling her by name. It was the old type all right, just like hers, yet this one had never been opened. It remained in its original package—a perfect, new brass doorknob—and it was had for just one dime.

Joyce wishes everyone could have such struggles at least once in their lifetime. She rejoices in the moments her family spent praying for a new pair of shoes, a new winter coat, or for dinner on the table. It was an opportunity to see God provide for His children, to see Him take interest in every last detail of their lives. Joyce understands that, with all her heart, God holds many gifts in His hands, riches greater than we can imagine. For in her time of need, God filled her home with special treasures, blessings in abundance, like a shiny, brass doorknob, more priceless than pure gold.

Friends Reunited

hey had been close, shared countless secrets, laughed and cried together. Teri Brinsley met Kelly in the 1980s, when they were both teens in a church youth group. They were friends for years, as close as sisters. They visited each other's homes, chatted for hours about their dreams for the future—wonderful husbands and children to call their own. On occasion, they'd utter a quiet prayer, lifting each other's needs into the mighty arms of God. But somehow, through life's twists and turns, the two had lost touch.

For more than a decade, Teri wondered about her friend. Then, in 1999, she began to pray. She asked God to help her find Kelly, to reunite them once more. Shortly afterwards, Teri was on a weekend excursion more than two hours from her home. She shopped in the lovely stores, looked at crafts, and enjoyed a quiet lunch. While walking down the tree-lined street, she heard a voice call her name. "Teri, is that you?" someone asked. Teri looked up and rejoiced. It was her dear friend Kelly. The two women hugged, exchanged phone numbers, and promised to keep in touch.

But even with the best intentions, a hectic life overwhelmed her. Teri's schedule wrapped itself around her as if attempting to choke every effort she made. A few months went by, and no calls had been made.

Then Teri had a dream. She saw her friend in horrible peril. She seemed to be drowning in raging waters. Teri cried out to her, and then she woke up. Without a doubt, she knew Kelly was in trouble. She rose from her bed and searched for her number. But where was it? Try as she might, Teri couldn't find it anywhere.

Desperate, she prayed: "Lord, I believe Kelly needs me. Please help me find her again." As if a light bulb had appeared in a cartoon, she suddenly remembered the name of Kelly's father's employer. She called the business and asked for him. Surely he would put her in touch with his daughter. When Teri dialed the number and spoke with the receptionist, she was told that Kelly's father had just suffered a heart attack. His family was with him at the hospital.

Now Teri understood her dream. She quickly drove to the hospital. Although she just missed Kelly, she was able to visit and pray with her friend's father before he went into surgery. Teri knew that God had led her there that day, and when word came back of the surgery's success, she thanked God for allowing her to be there for her friend.

Thanks to prayer and the warning in a dream, God had reunited these two women once more. With plans to get together soon and tender telephone chats, the two vow to never lose touch again. For they understand, better than most, that the gift of a true friend is heaven-sent.

A Future for Frank

or Brenda Ganz, 1987 was to be a year for new beginnings—a new town, a new state, a better life. Or so she
thought. Brenda had recently moved her family from
Wisconsin to California. But the golden state did not offer her all
she'd hoped it would. Her son, Frank, was in the fourth grade.
He'd always done well in school. He was never a problem. But this
time, things were different. He was having trouble adjusting.
Brenda's phone rang off the wall: calls in the morning, calls in the
afternoon, complaints about her son.

Week after week, she'd pick him up in the office. He'd been
fighting; he was not getting along. Try as she might, Brenda
couldn't understand what was wrong. He'd never been in trouble
before. Perhaps it was the adjustment—starting a new school,
making new friends, and moving so far away from home. She took
her boy aside and asked what was wrong. "The kids are bullying
me, Mom. They follow me around, looking for trouble. When they
hit me, I get blamed."

Weeks went by, and the calls kept coming. Brenda spent hours
in the principal's office trying to explain, trying to prove her son
was not who they thought he was. He was not a fighter. The principal was not so sure. He'd heard it all before. True, no one ever
saw the fights begin. They just had to make assumptions. Since
Frank was always involved, he must be responsible.

When Brenda couldn't wait any longer, she began to consider
private education. She wanted Frank to have a positive school
experience and to make friendships that would last a lifetime.

When Brenda attempted to enroll him, she hit a stumbling
block. The private school requested Frank's records. They were
not pleased. It seemed her son was a troublemaker. They couldn't
have his type in their school. He would just have to stay where he

was. Brenda tried to explain, realizing all the while that her pleas sounded like those of any mother who loved her son, any mother in denial. Silently she prayed, "Please help my son to have a good future."

Just then, a teacher entered the room. She recognized Frank. "I used to substitute at your school. You were being picked on all the time. I'm glad you made it out of there. I'm glad you'll be attending our school instead."

On those golden words, spoken at just the right moment, young Frank was admitted to his new school. He was given a second chance. He attended daily with no more problems and no more fights. His grades skyrocketed. He was one of their finest students.

Brenda is thankful for the opportunity her son was given. She's grateful that someone believed in him, just as a mother did. She knows that God sent that teacher, like an angel, carrying a message at just the right moment, to give her young son the life he deserved.

Frank is a grown man now. He's well educated, healthy, and strong. Recently, he married his childhood sweetheart, a girl he met at that very school while both were in the sixth grade.

On that dark and hopeless day, when Brenda cried out to God for Frank's future, she had no idea she was praying for a time far beyond graduation. For God's amazing answer included an extra blessing, a lovely wife for her son, a heavenly gift beyond earthly imagination.

A Sign in Nature

A baby to hold, to nurture, to call her own: this was Sandra Marks' dream. She'd prayed, tried to conceive, and then, frustrated, prayed some more. Each month she was crushed, left with no reason to purchase soft, delicate baby bonnets or to wear maternity blouses made by designers without imaginations.

Although taken with anticipation, each pregnancy test was negative. Soon, Sandra could bear it no longer. Then, in 1980, she read a book by a Native American author. Her writing, so descriptive, spoke of God's use of creation to show His children the way. Sometimes, she read, animal guides were used to help people—a part of creation doing the bidding of the Creator. Sandra's eyes began to open as they never had before. Her faith was restored, her prayer life renewed.

One afternoon, while crying out to God for an answer, Sandra begged for help. She could no longer have her hopes lifted, only to have them brought crashing down to reality. If she were pregnant, would God give her a clear sign in nature? Just then, furious barking from Sandra's cocker spaniel, Lizzy, interrupted her time of solitude. The noise grew louder and more persistent, until Sandra, annoyed at the intrusion, got off her knees and moved toward the sliding glass door and onto the patio. "Stop that barking!" Sandra ordered. But Lizzy would not comply. She barked louder and refused to come to attention. Exasperated, Sandra walked out into the yard to investigate what was the matter.

And then she saw it, a sign in nature, a promise from God. Within inches of her furiously barking dog sat a large brown owl. After a few minutes, the friendly visitor glanced her way, took flight over the fence, and soared out of the yard.

Now Sandra couldn't wait to take a pregnancy test, for she already knew the results. God had answered her prayers with a sign from nature. An owl in her suburban backyard, motionless before a barking dog, out of its time element in broad daylight, refusing to leave until she understood.

Her daughter was born several months later. The owl has never returned since. But Sandra knows from whence that bird came and the purpose for which he arrived. He was a gift from God's awesome nature, who brought good news, a promise of joy to her fragile and broken heart, sent from above, as an answer to prayer.

Believe

Their relationship was strong. It held all the elements of true friendship: trust, loyalty, and compassion. Becky Dittemore and Anne were never too busy to share a good laugh, to lend an ear, or to offer their hearts in times of need.

Over the years, Anne's faith had been tested. She had suffered great loss. She felt crushed by the weight of prayers gone unanswered. Her faith was broken, weak at best. Anne had forgotten what it was like to believe.

Becky, on the other hand, trusted in the goodness of God, of His supernatural intervention through prayer. She knew God cared and had compassion for our needs. But Becky's faith was soon to be tested.

As Becky drove down the highway near her home, she saw the evidence of a horrible accident: emergency crews everywhere, a totaled car, and an unknown patient being taken by life flight to a nearby hospital. Sorrow struck Becky's heart as she prayed for the victim, prayed for recovery, and prayed for the loved ones who would soon be notified.

Then Becky heard the news. Anne called, terrified and in a panic. Her 16-year-old daughter, Amy, had been in a horrible accident. Her car had been struck; not everyone had survived. She'd been taken by life flight to a trauma center. Things did not look good.

The first few days at the hospital were touch-and-go. The doctors told Anne to expect the worst. No mother wants to say goodbye, to anticipate the loss of her child, but Anne was forced to prepare herself for that horrible possibility. She tried desperately to pray, but the words wouldn't come.

Becky put her faith into practice. She would believe for her friend, be the strength for her weakness. Each morning, while she prepared breakfast, she lifted Amy's needs in prayer. Then, in faith, she took the heavy burden and placed it directly before the throne of God. Each evening, she'd pray once more: for Amy's healing, for strength, and for recovery.

As months went by, Becky offered all she could: someone to talk to, someone to care, and someone to believe. But, in spite of her prayers, Amy remained in a coma, lost in a world of distance, unreachable to everyone.

Anne stayed by her daughter's side night and day, watching over her, brushing her hair, talking to her softly, and offering a mother's unquenchable love. But, as hard as she tried, Anne couldn't pray. Each time she attempted, she became paralyzed by fear, by memories of prayers that seemed unanswered, and of loss too great to grasp.

One afternoon, Becky heard distant church bells chime. Oh, she'd heard them before, but this time it was different. The bells seemed to call her name, to beckon her outside, down the street, and into the sanctuary. Becky stopped what she was doing, walked toward the bells, and stepped inside the chapel. As she entered the door, her heart leaped with faith. With the clear determination of a woman understanding her purpose, Becky knelt and began to pray. But this time her prayers were different. She did not pray for Amy. Instead, her heart and soul reached out to Anne. The presence in the room was powerful: everything in her senses cried out, "Believe."

When Becky left the chapel, she headed straight for a phone. "Anne, I don't know the answers. I don't know why these horrible events happened. Life can be difficult; you know that's true. I wish I could promise that Amy will recover, but I can't. I only know one thing: no matter what happens, Annie, you must believe."

Anne hesitated for a moment; the telephone fell silent. It was difficult to take a chance, to hope, to believe once more. But she promised to give it a try. When she left Amy's room that night, she would attempt to pray. Anne would try to believe.

The next morning, Becky's telephone rang. When she picked it up, she heard the excited voice of her dear friend. It was a miracle! She had believed, and God had seen them through. Amy had awakened from her coma! The two women rejoiced together; laughing and crying all at the same time. Anne had prayed and God had listened. Amy was back — her young daughter was coming home.

There was still much work to do, but with therapy and time, Amy soon recovered. Today she's bright and healthy, and she continues to be the joy of her mother's heart. Becky and Anne remain dear friends. Their souls are closer than ever, entwined by an experience that binds them for eternity.

And to this day, when they hear church bells chime, the two women stop, take a moment, and thank God. They thank Him for Amy's life, for answers to prayer, for faith renewed, and, most of all, for teaching them both what it means to "Believe."

The Prayer Journal

Kristi kept one for years: a journal to share her secret thoughts, her heart, and her prayers with God. From time to time, she would read back through the pages, over the passages, reminding herself where she'd been, what she'd come through, and where now, in faith, she was going.

As she grew into a young woman, her prayer journal took on a new tone. Kristi prayed for a future husband—not just any spouse, but one sent specifically by the Lord. She desired a man who was strong and kind, faithful and loving, and who had a deep love and respect for God. For Kristi, it was clear that nothing less would do.

It was Christmas 1994. The crisp California air was filled with the hope of the season. The smell of sweet cinnamon filled Kristi's childhood home. The family tree shone brightly, beckoning visitors inside. With soft, colored lights twinkling on the rooftop, and mistletoe hung in the doorway, Christmas was on its way.

During the holidays, Kristi was introduced to a young man. When she first saw Damian Voiles, something inside her sensed he was different. He had a certain strength about him, a tenderness that she had never encountered before. That evening, the young couple went out and had a wonderful time. Kristi felt so comfortable around Damian that she couldn't help wondering if he might be the one. When she returned from her date, she sat down and quietly wrote in her journal, "I believe tonight I may have met my future husband."

Kristi knew Damian was the kind of man she could easily fall in love with. But her feelings were so fragile, so delicate that she didn't want to be hurt, to be crushed and disappointed. Kristi asked God to wrap a shroud of protection around her heart. If Damian was not the one, she wanted to keep him at arm's length. If he was the man for her, Kristi asked God to show her a clear sign of assurance. Kristi prayed, wrote in her journal, and then waited.

Over the next few months, the couple continued to date, but Damian showed no real signs of commitment. On Valentine's Day, after Kristi had asked God for a sign, Damian tenderly kissed Kristi on the forehead. "Could this be my sign?" she wondered.

Not wanting to become too involved, Kristi decided to get on with her life. If God wanted them together, God knew where to find her. She enrolled in a Bible college on the East Coast—a school thousands of miles from home, thousands of miles away from Damian Voiles.

While at school, she dated others. Many were fine young men, but no one compared to Damian. Kristi's journal continued to grow, page by page filled with soul-searching prayer after soul-searching prayer. At times, discouraged and heartbroken, she wondered if God existed at all.

Before she knew it, the Christmas season was once again upon her. Kristi traveled home to see her family, to celebrate Christ's birth, to smell the sweet cinnamon, to view the soft, twinkling lights, and to help decorate the festive family tree.

Within a few days, Damian heard she was in town. He called and asked Kristi out on a date. Filled with both anticipation and fear, she agreed. "Dear God, please don't let me get hurt. You know how much I care for Damian, but I want him to feel the same about me."

Kristi put on her prettiest dress, brushed her hair, and dabbed on her favorite perfume. As she headed out the door, she silently prayed. "Please God, if Damian's the one, let him say that he needs me in his life."

Later that evening, Damian took her aside. He told Kristi she was special. Then he said what she longed to hear: "I believe God is showing me that I need you in my life." No other words were necessary. Kristi had her confirmation—Damian was the one.

In time, an engagement was set, and a wedding soon followed. Kristi's hopes and dreams had come true. God had given her the desire of her heart: a man with strength, kindness, love, and a deep faith in God.

Before the wedding, Kristi shared her journal with Damian, prayers written from the heart of a young woman seeking God's plan for a husband-to-be. Together they read, and they both understood, that God had been faithful.

Someday, when the Voileses are blessed with children, they will once again share Kristi's prayer journal. The words, so eloquently written, will teach their children of God's faithfulness, of His goodness in bringing their parents together. As they read along, they'll hear the story and learn much more than photo albums could portray. They'll discover, in their mother's journal, a young woman's faith in God, the sacred source of abundant blessings in their happy home.

A Gift for Valentine's Day

No gift is more precious, none is so sacred, as the birth of a new baby. Through good times and bad, they're in our hearts and lives forever.

Sarah Carleson's sister, Felicia, was pregnant. Times were tough. Felicia was separated from her husband; this would be her first child. In the autumn of 1979, Sarah took her sister in, offered the warmth of family, a home, and a comforting ear. The two spent time together, reminiscing about their childhood, their own individual struggles, and their hopes and dreams for the baby-to-be. "Things will get better," Sarah assured her. "You'll see. Together, we'll make it through."

On Valentine's Day, 1980, Raakhee was born, a beautiful baby in every way, with huge brown eyes that captured everyone's hearts. Family came from all around. Together they rejoiced. Surely, with this birth, things were bound to get better.

But they did not. The next day, with flowers in hand and excitement in her step, Sarah arrived at the hospital. As she walked down several long hallways, she found medical staff surrounding the tiny newborn. "What's wrong?" she asked in a panic. The doctor took her aside and quietly offered grim news. Raakhee, healthy only the day before, was experiencing unexplained seizures. The tiny newborn would have to be transferred to a nearby research facility. Before Sarah knew it, Raakhee was bundled up, whisked down a corridor, and placed in an ambulance, on her way to Stanford Hospital.

Sarah and Felicia were devastated. Raakhee was critically ill, and no one could tell them why. Sarah tried to offer her sister comfort. The baby would be all right; the doctors would discover what was wrong. But deep down inside, Sarah wasn't so sure.

Sarah and Felicia, although not usually driven to prayer, were motivated by desperate circumstances. Together they had to have faith; it was their only hope. Frantic, they went in search of the nearest chapel.

As they climbed the steps of the sanctuary and opened the huge, wooden double doors, Sarah and Felicia felt a sacred, holy presence. The two women lit candles and then solemnly knelt to pray. The sisters prayed as they never had before. "Raakhee is so young, so innocent. Please heal her small, fragile body."

Sarah and Felicia were determined to see an answer, determined to experience a miracle. And a miracle is what they received. Just days later, through the echoes of Christ's name, Sarah and Felicia saw a sign—the very fingerprints of God. Baby Raakhee began to recover. Her vital signs improved, and the horrible seizures stopped. When she was released from the hospital, everyone rejoiced.

Many years have come and gone, but with each Valentine's Day that passes, Sarah and Felicia stop and thank God. They thank Him for faith renewed, for answers to prayer, and for the continuing bond between them. But most of all, as they light the candles upon the cake, they thank God for the healthy young woman whose birthday they're about to celebrate.

The Older Brother

A big, strong older brother, someone to count on, to lean on in times of trouble. Matt Johnson had always watched over his little sister, Karen, since the day she was born in 1961. With more than 10 years between them, he'd taken on the role of protector since she was old enough to toddle into the kitchen and empty pots and pans onto the floor. When Karen began school, Matt walked with her, making sure she arrived safely. At 3:00, he'd be there waiting, just like clockwork, to make the journey home again. Matt would do anything for Karen—after all, that's what big brothers were for.

Many years came and went. The two grew, married, and had children of their own. Matt moved to Virginia, and Karen remained in California. They continued to keep in touch, sending cards and notes and exchanging timely phone calls.

Sometimes, life changes our perspective, moves us in different directions than any of us would expect. Over the years, Karen developed a drinking problem. In her heart, she knew that she was not raising her two young children the way she should. Karen wanted to be a good example for her young ones, the kind of example her parents had been for her. But try as she might, she couldn't seem to stop. So, in the spring of 1999, Karen called her older brother, Matt.

As big brothers will do, without hesitation, he scheduled a visit to California. He thought they might take long afternoon walks and look back on their childhoods. He took time off from work, made plane reservations, and kissed his family good-bye.

While waiting for his plane, he decided to kill a little time and grab a book at the airport gift shop. He found an inspirational title about family relationships. This was just what he needed. He grabbed a cup of coffee, picked up the book, and boarded the plane. Once the plane had taken off—patchwork landscape beneath them, clear skies ahead— Matt reclined his chair in a comfortable position and began to read. Much to his surprise, this was not just a book about relationships, but about the effects of alcohol on the family unit, and about the impact of faith on our lives. This was the perfect book to share with Karen. He read non-stop throughout the flight, gleaning wonderful insight for his sister. Just as the plane taxied, Matt finished the last page.

When he saw Karen, they hugged, laughed, and cried. It had been a few years since their last visit. How he missed his little sister. Matt settled into a guest room in Karen's home, unpacked his bags, and said a prayer. "Please, God, give me the right words to help Karen. You know how much I love her, but I know You love her more. Please show me what I can do to help."

That evening, Karen's husband stayed with the kids while Matt and his sister went out to dinner. They wanted to catch up on their lives, to have the chance to be alone and share their hearts, the secrets from deep inside. While they sat in a local cafe, Matt and Karen discussed her drinking problem. His sister wanted to stop, but she couldn't seem to find the strength to do it by herself. Karen's children were important to her. How could she create the good example, the kind of home she and Matt had been so fortunate to grow up in? Although Matt believed that God was Karen's answer, he silently prayed for wisdom, for the right words to touch her heart.

Just then, a young man came into the cafe. He sat next to them, and within moments, the three struck up a conversation. They casually discussed their hometowns, their childhood, their families. The young man proudly spoke of his parents and the strong influence their faith had on his upbringing. He told Matt and Karen that without his mom and dad's strong Christian beliefs, he didn't know how he would have made it through life's constant ups and downs. As the young man spoke, Matt's words were confirmed, and Karen's heart was touched. She knew it was true: she must put her problems into the strong hands of God, to be a better person, to be the kind of mom, the kind of example, she longed to be.

A few days later, Matt hugged his sister good-bye, told her he loved her, and said that he would continue praying for her recovery. He left that day knowing that God had heard his prayers. He had given Karen the right words, only words not spoken from his lips. He had brought a young man, a stranger, like an angel, to speak to her heart at just the right moment. God was watching over Karen, and a great burden was lifted from Matt's shoulders.

Karen is still recovering. She daily reaches out to God for the strength she needs, for the comfort only He can offer. Matt continues to be there for his younger sister, to call her, to soothe her fears, and, of course, to pray. After all, that's what big brothers are for.

The Promise

Pregnant! Mary Testerman and her husband were having a baby. She was thrilled. Maternity clothes were fitted, baby clothes and furniture were carefully purchased. Ever since she was a young girl, Mary had longed for tiny babies of her own. Her lifelong dream for a family was about to come true. It was clear: 1984 was going to be Mary's year. Relatives rejoiced; friends threw her baby showers. Mary couldn't have been happier.

When she was full-term and the labor pains arrived, loved ones gathered around. They sat patiently, drinking coffee with joy in their hearts as they waited to greet the newest member of their happy clan. When the tiny newborn arrived, they named her Stefanie Nicole. Mary gazed at her little angel with bundles of love. This was how it was supposed to be, how she'd always dreamed.

While the baby rested in the nursery, loved ones filed into Mary's room one by one. They brought her flowers and gifts, and they congratulated her with hugs. When Mary's grandmother arrived at her bedside, the two women embraced. But suddenly her grandmother turned pale, quietly excused herself, and left the room. "What was the matter?" Mary wondered.

Although Stefanie Nicole appeared healthy at birth, she took a sudden turn for the worst and tragically died 18 hours later. Mary was devastated. Her family and friends were in shock. Mary's grandmother was notified. The baby was gone—Mary's newborn baby had tragically died. Her grandmother grew quiet and then began to speak. At the hospital, while at Mary's bedside, she had seen a vision. She saw the image of Jesus, and He had spoken to her. He told her that Stefanie was sick and that He must soon take her to heaven. Then He made a promise. He promised that Mary would have more children. Then the grandmother shared more. During the night, tiny Stefanie had come to her room. She had rocked the dying baby, until she passed from this world into heaven.

When no one seemed to believe her, thinking these merely the words of an old, confused woman, the grandmother began to describe the newborn in detail. She mentioned a patch of missing hair. Then, and only then, was she believed. Stefanie's hair had been partially shaven to allow for the I.V.

Her grandmother's work had just begun. Mary was seriously depressed. She had lost her child, so soon after birth and with no warning of illness, nothing to prepare her for the loss. Her grandmother explained that it was all right to be angry, that God understood. But she told Mary that she must never give up, never lose her faith. She would have more children.

In time, Mary conceived again, and with fear in heart, she tried to believe. Perhaps this child would be hers to keep. But, as time would tell, it was not. This child also died, leaving Mary desperate, alone, and afraid. This time, her depression was so deep, so dark, even her grandmother's words of comfort could no longer pull her out of the shadowy abyss.

In 1986, when Mary became pregnant for the third time, terror struck her soul. No matter how hard she tried to believe her doctors, to believe her grandmother, Mary was unable to trust again. She could not have hope, could not be so utterly destroyed one more time.

Desperate, her grandmother reached out to God. For seven days she went to church, knelt down, and begged God for help. If God could show her His promise, why couldn't He show Mary? Her granddaughter's faith was at stake. It had been shattered to pieces, and only God had the ability to restore it once again. "Please God," she pleaded. "Please, show Mary what you've shown me. Please give her back her faith."

On the seventh day, Mary lay in her bed. Restless, she tossed and turned until she'd cried herself to sleep. While in a slumber,

Mary had a vision. First she saw her grandmother. She brought Mary to a beautiful place with massive doors that were difficult to open. Mary tried and tried, and when the doors finally gave way, she walked inside. There, Mary saw herself at a distance. She was holding a baby, and another baby was snuggled in a blanket at the foot of her bed. Close by, she saw a beautiful figure, a person Mary believed to be the Lord. Then they told her that the baby in her arms was the daughter she was now pregnant with. The baby at the foot of the bed was her next child, a son. Mary was given a promise that both children would live, but she must make a vow. After this vision, Mary must promise to let go of the fear in her heart and trust in what she'd seen and heard. Then her grandmother said, "Are you OK now?" When Mary nodded, she added, "Then keep your promise and be happy."

When Mary awoke, she couldn't wait to call her grandmother. It was only then that Mary learned of her weeklong prayers offered for the gift of restored faith.

The pregnancy had its ups and downs, but just as the vision promised, her daughter was born, alive and healthy. Then, just four years later, in 1990, Mary became pregnant again, and a healthy young son joined their family.

Mary knows that life can be filled with struggles, with devastation, with unanswered questions. But she learned from her grandmother to never lose sight of her faith, for God is her comforter and the giver of life. When problems and doubts return, Mary needs only to look at her two beautiful children to be assured it's still true.

A Teddy Bear Christmas

I t was December 1990, and Teri's daughters, Shelbie and Kristen, were spending their first weekend away from home. They would stay with a family friend, an exciting plan for two giggly girls ages five and three. Teri carefully packed their bags with toothbrushes, play clothes, toys, and warm winter coats. With a tender kiss and a quick "I love you," she sent them on their way.

The fragrance of Christmas filled the crisp winter air. Teri decided to use her time wisely. Why spend it moping around the house? She was determined to make each moment count. She grabbed her purse and headed to a nearby department store. There she'd fill her heart with the joy of the season, as she carefully chose the perfect gifts for her children.

Teri purchased soft velour slippers and bright red pajamas. She selected cuddly brown bears that were perfect for rocking in little girls' arms. What a wonderful Christmas this would be.

Around 3:00 in the afternoon, Teri was suddenly caught by surprise with a deep, knowing feeling, a desperate sense of urgency. Something was wrong with her children. Teri knew, without a shadow of a doubt, that one of her daughters was in danger. In the middle of the store, she stopped, bowed her head, and silently prayed for their safety: "Lord, wherever Shelbie and Kristen may be, please watch over them, protect them, and bring them safely home." Then, with the peace that passes all understanding, she raised her head and headed out the door.

Teri clutched her packages and turned up her collar. She fought the wind and ran for her car. As she drove home, she breathed a sigh of relief. Teri was certain that her children were safe. Whatever had been wrong, God was in control.

On Sunday, when her daughters returned home again, running up the steps and into her arms, Teri asked Shelbie about their weekend. As the story unfolded, Teri began to shudder. On Saturday, around 3:00, Kristen had been lost in a crowded shopping mall. The mall was filled with holiday shoppers. How would they ever find her? They had searched everywhere, up and down the aisles, through store after store, only to find her twenty minutes later. The toddler had tried to go outside, but fortunately she couldn't open the heavy doors. Finally, a kind man brought her to an information booth where they were all reunited.

Teri hugged her children and rejoiced in God's goodness. She thanked Him for the warning and for His protective wings that surrounded them with love.

Yes, this Christmas would be a special one, thanks to God's answer to prayer, with Shelbie and Kristen resting soundly in their beds, wearing bright red pajamas and rocking teddy bears in their arms.

The Birthday Gift

It was September 30, 1999, and Cynthia Chamberlain's forty-fourth birthday. For the most part, she expected a regular sort of day. Gone were the years of giddy anticipation, balloons, loud music, cheers, or fancy gifts. As time went on, the celebration became more subdued, much quieter, a simple occasion. All she desired was a piece of cake, a cup of hot coffee, and family members gathered by her side. What more could any woman want for her birthday?

Cynthia's son, Matthew, was 25. He had recently purchased a shiny new motorcycle. Like all young men who never quite outgrow their fascination with bikes, Matthew treated the motorcycle as his pride and joy. Yet even though her son was an adult now, with a wife and home of his own, Cynthia still worried. She had spent Matthew's childhood tending to cut knees and elbows: a little medicine, a little Band-Aid, and a big kiss from Mom to make it all better. But a motorcycle was different. Cynthia took comfort in the fact that Matthew was not the reckless type. He wore a helmet and drove safely. Still, as a mother will, she worried, and she prayed. She asked God to protect her son, to send guardian angels to watch over him.

On the afternoon of Cynthia's birthday, Matthew rode down the street. As he followed a tree-lined path, God watched over him from heaven, and angels flanked his sides. Suddenly, Matthew's motorcycle was struck by car. He was thrown into oncoming traffic. Matthew was unable to stand, unable to walk. He was forced to roll into the gutter to avoid being hit again and again. His prized motorcycle lay totaled, in pieces upon the roadside.

Within moments, the ambulance arrived. They rushed him to a local trauma center. Matthew's wife was on her way. His mother had just been notified. When they arrived at the hospital,

Matthew's wife looked pale. She had just driven past the accident sight. The motorcycle was crushed beyond recognition. What horrible condition might Matthew be in?

First, his wife was escorted into the room. Then Cynthia reluctantly followed. What she expected is not what she saw. Matthew was only slightly bruised: no blood, no horrible injuries. They talked, they laughed, and Cynthia cried.

When Matthew spoke, he shared something that occurred as he lay in the gutter. Matthew had heard the voice of God. He had been given a stern warning. He was never to ride a motorcycle again. Matthew made a vow, and Cynthia rested in knowing her son is good to his word.

While doctors and nurses scrambled about, they continued to shake their heads in amazement. "No one comes into the trauma center after an accident like Matthew's in his condition. Your son should be dead." They checked the X-rays over and over, sure they were missing something. But they were not. Soon the doctors released Matthew with a clean bill of health: no broken bones, no permanent damage, only a few bruises to testify of his brush with death.

Matthew took his mother in his arms and offered an apology. "I'm sorry this happened on your birthday, Mom. I don't have a present for you."

Cynthia sighed with relief. "A present!" she laughed. "I've been given the greatest present a mother can receive. God has answered my prayers. I have a gift beyond all others; my son's alive and well!"

What more could any mother want for her birthday?

Psalm 81:10

For it was I, your God, who brought you out of the land of Egypt. Only test me, open your mouth wide, and see if I won't fill it. You will receive every blessing you can use.

Only days before, Marta Marquez heard the sermon based on Psalm 81:10. The scripture had touched her heart, inspired her, and given her hope. She was sure of one thing: God is willing and able to provide for His children. Marta, a young mother of three, was open to miracles, and that day a miracle was exactly what she needed.

It was 1979, and her youngest son, Carlos, was only a few months old. Marta had just fed Carlos the last drop of formula. As Marta searched the pantry, it was clear that their supply had completely run dry. With her son's feeding time rapidly approaching, the young mom began to panic.

Marta's family was struggling at the time, trying their best to make ends meet. They had survived, like many others, from paycheck to paycheck. But now that paycheck was a day away, and her innocent baby couldn't wait.

Marta set out to solve the problem in the only way she knew how: she prayed. She asked God to provide for Carlos, to care for him as one of His own. Then she asked Him for another favor: "God, I need encouragement. Please help me find that scripture from the sermon I recently heard. I have no idea where in the Bible to look."

In faith, Marta opened the Holy Book, and it fell open to the Psalms. She had read only a few verses when, sure enough, she saw it: "Only test me. Open your mouth wide and see if I won't fill it." That was her answer! It was a sign, the found scripture, a promise of provision.

As Marta wrapped Carlos in a soft blue blanket, she gently rocked him to sleep. With each swaying motion, she continued to pray. "Please take care of my baby. Please provide for him just like your scripture promises." In faith, Marta waited. Then she began to wonder. How would God provide? Would He send formula from a kind benefactor? How would He fill the mouth of this tiny, hungry baby?"

Hours went by, and Carlos continued to rest, undisturbed, in a peaceful slumber. Concerned by his sudden change in feeding schedule, Marta entered her baby's room. She checked on him and observed an answer to prayer: not her usual hungry infant, but a resting, quiet angel, with a distended, full tummy. When Carlos awoke the next morning, he was smiling, happy, refusing even a bottle of warm water.

That afternoon, Marta's husband returned from work. He had cashed his paycheck and carried armfuls of baby formula. Then, and only then, did her tiny son appear hungry. Marta fed Carlos with joy as she offered thanks for God's faithfulness.

Today, as she reflects back over the years, Marta remains grateful for a promise in scripture, for the tender filling of her young child, and because God continues to provide her family with "every blessing they can use."

Feed the Birds

Every morning, Alex Schneider would go to his kitchen window and feed the birds. Carefully, he'd tear small pieces of stale bread, an offering for his feathered friends. It was a time-honored tradition. Each sunrise, as if by engraved invitation, the small creatures would wait for him, eat their meal, and then sing him a thank-you song.

When World War II was in full force, Alex was sent to France. He didn't want to leave his wife, Heidi, and his three young daughters. He worried for their safety. But there was no choice. He, like many others, was sent away into an unknown future. His wife did her best to make life appear normal. She kept her children busy, offering the extra hugs and kisses they'd miss from their father. Each day, the family prayed for his safe return. Months would pass, often without word. They never knew if their loved one was alive or dead.

Heidi steadfastly continued her husband's tradition. Each morning, she would take stale bread, break it into small pieces, go to the kitchen window, and offer breakfast to the birds. Only now, a new creature began to arrive. Each morning, a beautiful white dove would perch itself on the windowsill and quietly eat its meal. Heidi thanked God for the dove. She knew he was a sign that her husband was still alive.

Each morning as she rose from bed, she offered a prayer for Alex and a prayer that the dove would return once more, a sign of reassurance that life for her family would go on. Every morning, without fail, the white dove arrived, greeted her with hope, ate his meal, then flew away.

When the war ended and Alex returned home, the family rejoiced. They rejoiced to see him alive; they rejoiced to be together once more. On the first morning, after his homecoming, he rose early, broke some bread, and brought it to the kitchen window. The beautiful birds, once again, gathered to see their old friend. They sang him a song, nibbled their meal, and then they flew away.

But among all the birds, there was no sign of the dove. Never again did he return to the window. His mission had been fulfilled, his comfort no longer needed. For their loved one was home, and the faithful white dove had flown back to heaven where he truly belonged.

Angel in the Garden

With soft, flowing hair, like strands of golden honey, Kathleen Treanor's four-year-old daughter, Ashley, was her mother's pride and joy. It was the springtime of 1995, a warm, sunny day; life was renewed. Mother and daughter drove to the local nursery to purchase a kit for a beautiful water garden. The two cherished nature and loved to watch flowers bloom with magnificent glory.

But today there was no time for gardening. A young mother's life is so busy, their project would have to wait for another afternoon. It had been a busy year for the Treanors. Kathleen spent endless hours in the car, driving to work and home again. There never seemed to be enough time for what she really wanted to do. Her heart's desire was to spend countless moments snuggling with her three children. She longed to read nursery rhymes, bake cookies, and yes, even plant water gardens. But, for now, those things would have to wait.

Everyone was rushing to get to soccer practice. Kathleen said, "Hurry kids, put on your uniforms: ready, set, go!" It was in the car, while on the way, that Ashley asked the question.

"Mommy, would you be sad if I died?"

Shocked, Kathleen answered, "I'd be terribly sad, Ashley. I'd miss you so much."

"But why, Mommy? I'd be with Jesus in heaven. I'd be an angel watching over you," Ashley comforted her mother.

"Yes, but in my heart, I'd miss you. I need my angel here with me."

That night, after she'd tucked her last child into bed, Kathleen wondered about their conversation. What had possessed Ashley to speak of such things? Soon she dismissed the thoughts.

Exhausted, she joined her husband, Mike, under soft blankets, where she fell into a deep sleep.

The sound of her alarm clock jolted Kathleen out of bed. While the two boys got ready for school, Kathleen tried to rouse Ashley from her sleep. Unlike her usual self, on this morning she resisted getting up. Ashley begged her mom to stay home from work, to stay home and play games. Kathleen would have given anything to do just that. But she had a new job. She had to be a responsible adult.

Kathleen dressed her little girl in comfortable tennis shoes, soft jeans, and an angel T-shirt. She pulled her hair back into a pony-tail and added pink ribbons. Then she drove Ashley to her in-laws' home. Mike's parents were wonderful people. They had embraced Kathleen into their family when she married their son and accepted her children as Mike's own. With a kiss good-bye and several hugs for the road, Kathleen left Ashley in their care.

She got to her office promptly at 8:00. At 9:02, it happened. It was a horrendous sound, an explosion that seemed to rock the city—Oklahoma City. The entire staff ran to the window. Black smoke filled the sky. Where was it coming from? What could have happened? Someone turned on the television. The local news reporters were there first. An explosion had occurred at the Alfred P. Murrah Federal Building. People were trapped inside. Rescue workers were just arriving. Young, desperate mothers were franti-cally running up and down the streets in search of their children.

"My God, there was a day care inside that building!" Kathleen gasped.

Then she silently prayed: a prayer for the dead, a prayer for the wounded, and a prayer for the families whose grief she could never understand. Kathleen wondered what it must be like. What would she do if one of her children were trapped inside? Suddenly, the office phone rang. It was her sister.

"Where is Ashley?" the panicked voice asked.

"She's with her grandparents."

"Kathleen, Mike's parents had an appointment with the Department of Social Security today."

Kathleen was attempting to soak it all in. What was her sister trying to tell her?

"Kathleen, you've got to find Ashley. The Social Security Department is inside the Alfred P. Murrah Federal Building!"

"Oh my God! Not Ashley, not my little girl! She can't be in that building!"

Everything after that was a blur: the distinct humming in her ears and the swirling images of people, shadows, and voices.

It would be a couple of days before they knew for sure. Then Kathleen and Mike received a call from the medical examiner's office. Their family was to come downtown right away. When they arrived, they were quickly escorted into a private office.

"I'm sorry," Mike and Kathleen were told, "but your daughter was found among the dead."

That's all she remembers. Her grief was too deep, too dark to comprehend. It washed over her soul like a flood, then emerged into loud groanings, a voice she hardly recognized as her own.

The next few days were a whirlwind: a memorial, a funeral, and the media constantly at her door. Little Ashley was gone, like so many other innocent people, because of evil hearts bent on a savage intent.

Kathleen would never fully understand why. No one would. But she rested in the comfort that only God could offer. She prayed for peace, she prayed for understanding, and she prayed that God would lift her out of a deep, dark pit of despair.

Soon, thoughts of having another child filled Kathleen's heart. After Ashley's birth, she'd had a tubal ligation. When she had first married Mike, they'd discussed having the procedure reversed. Now Kathleen longed for another baby. She understood clearly that no child could ever replace Ashley. But to give life once more, to hold another infant in her arms, would bring joy back to her wounded soul.

The procedure was costly, more expensive than they could afford. Although an offer was made to do the surgery for free in New Jersey, Kathleen didn't want to leave her husband and two sons. Mike felt that if it were meant to be, if they should have another child, the operation would be performed by Kathleen's own doctor, right in Oklahoma City. Kathleen prayed, "If it is Your will, God, please work out the details and do it in such a way that I know the answer is from You."

A few days later, Mike's insurance company added a clause to their policy. They would cover the surgery one time and one time only. Kathleen and her husband had their answer. Although the odds for success were only 50 percent, they were given hope, a chance for another child. The operation was performed on Kathleen's birthday, the greatest present she could have received.

Although Kathleen met each month with anticipation, every passing day brought her more crushing disappointment. After two years of trying, two years of hoping, Kathleen put her dream into God's hands: "If I never have another child, Lord, I am grateful for the time I had with Ashley, and I'm grateful for two healthy sons. I want to live in peace with whatever Your plan is for my life."

Just a few weeks later, on Father's Day, she found out. God had chosen to bless them. The test was positive! They were expecting a baby. The heaviness of life seemed to lift like a curtain, allowing light, once again, into her soul.

Little Kassidy Caitlin came into the world on February 17, 1999. She has brought joy to the Treanor household, brought peace to her mother's existence.

There's a special place in Kathleen's heart reserved just for Ashley. But, through the grace of God, through the gift of another child, this young mother is finally able to rejoin the living.

Recently, Kathleen planted Ashley's water garden with vibrant flowers, a trickling pond, and cascading weeping willow trees. Just as sure as a little angel watches from heaven, down here on earth, Ashley's garden still blooms.

Matchmaker

Everything was different here: the language, the people, the landscape. America was nothing like Yvonne's homeland in Germany. But it was the mid-1980s, and this young woman was on an adventure. Yvonne had recently started a job as a nanny for the small child of a young California couple. The job was great—the home beautiful, the sweet, little boy adorable—but Yvonne missed her friends terribly. She had left her personal life behind. Feeling lost and lonely, Yvonne prayed for a companion.

One afternoon, her employer made a suggestion. Why not run a personal ad in the paper? Yvonne could advertise for someone to spend time with on her free evenings from work. There was nothing to worry about, she was assured. Just some casual, fun dates out on the town. What could possibly be wrong with that? Now, Yvonne had seen this type of ad before. In Europe, this was a common practice, but still she wasn't certain. What sort of people might she attract? Surely she would not find her soul mate in the want ads.

Over the next few days, she was persuaded. The ad was called in, and soon it ran in the local paper: "Lonely German girl seeking companionship." Yvonne was shocked at the large response. One hundred and eleven letters, to be exact. Some were from fine young men, some literally from criminals writing from inside the walls of the state penitentiary. It took all kinds to find her prince.

For some time, Gordon Sholz had been busy working nights in the grocery industry. His unusual schedule made it difficult to meet people. Feeling lonely, he prayed that God would send him a suitable companion.

Soon after, on a quiet morning, as he turned the pages of the local newspaper, he discussed his dream girl with a friend. "My mom is from Germany," he reasoned. "Perhaps I'll find a German girl in the personal ads."

Against all odds, as he searched through the paper, there was the perfect ad—Yvonne's ad: "Lonely German girl seeking companionship." Gordon felt certain she was the one. Immediately, he wrote to Yvonne. The two met and hit it off right away. They felt as if they had known each other for a lifetime; they were so close, had so much in common. Within a year they married in a small, private ceremony.

Gordon and Yvonne recently celebrated their fourteenth wedding anniversary. Today they have two beautiful, fair-haired sons and a wonderful, happy marriage. They live together in a charming new home in Northern California.

Gordon's and Yvonne's destiny began with prayer, then a dream come true: a lonely German girl who turned out to be just the one.

A Home for Charles

Triplets. Alice Fields' mother was having triplets! This kind of thing didn't happen every day. Alice's family was special. They were blessed.

It was 1954, and Alice had just turned three. She was far too young to understand what went wrong in that Southern California delivery room. The triplets' birth had been complicated. One baby died, and Charles was born with cerebral palsy. The mood in her home went from joyous anticipation to quiet despair.

But Alice loved her twin brothers, Charles and Fred. She was as close as any sister can be to two rambunctious young boys. Together they'd make lemonade, put together a stand, and collect nickels and dimes for a new toy. They'd play for hours in their large backyard: "Tag, you're it." They were a team, Alice and her brothers.

Then in 1959, when Charles was five, he contracted polio, another disability to complicate his life. Alice watched in disbelief as her little brother was taken from their family home and placed in a large institution. Perhaps for some it seemed the right thing to do, but Alice knew better.

Charles came home on the weekends. Each Saturday morning, Alice was sent inside the institution to pick him up. No one else in her family could bear the sight, the smell, of that awful asylum. Alice, only eight, would run for young Charles, grab his things, throw them in a bag, and wheel him quickly toward the door, out of that place, away from where he didn't belong. Each night, as she said her prayers, she asked God to show her the way, to show her how to help Charles.

During his weekend visits home, she listened as her five-year-old brother would plot his escape, a way out of that terrible place. Each time she convinced him to stay put, to wait, to be brave. Someday, she would get him out. God would show her the way.

Many years came and went, and Alice kept her vow. She wanted a place that smelled like baked cookies, that had real linens on the beds and colorful prints on the wall. And, just like always, Charles's big sister came through.

In 1979, Alice found the perfect California care home. Charles's new place was everything Alice had prayed for, everything her younger brother deserved. It was a small care home, designed for six, with a loving, gentle staff and a warm, friendly atmosphere. When Charles arrived and unpacked his bags, he could hardly believe it was true. He was actually staying, and for more than a few days. Charles was grateful for a home.

One weekend, the staff took him to the Rose Parade. A group of six wrapped in wool blankets and camped out in wheelchairs, drinking cocoa while they reserved the perfect spot to see the floats. Charles was grateful for a hot beverage, a warm blanket, and for a good seat at the parade.

Two years later, he went to the beach, a man of 27, weighing 275 pounds, lifted from his wheelchair by two assistants and carried through the sand to the waves. He was so grateful to be there, so astounded at the ocean he'd only seen in pictures, that he cried.

Today, Charles holds no resentments for his past, for his disabilities, or for choices others made that cost him so much. Charles has no time for that. He is too busy being grateful for what he has now: for a home, for friends, and for his big sister, Alice, who came through after all.

To Reap and to Sow

V.L. Walker grew up in Mississippi in the 1920s with nine siblings—six brothers and three sisters. Along with his family, he worked as a sharecropper on a large farm. They raised beans, cabbage, tomatoes—the best produce around. Food was exchanged for labor, but the land belonged to someone else. His family dreamed of owning their own farm, but that possibility seemed beyond their reach. Life was rough, times were hard; they were grateful for the opportunities they had.

V.L. and his siblings worked hard, out in the fields in the blazing hot sun. There was no time for nonsense like bickering or petty jealousy. They had to survive, and it took all their unified energy to make that possible.

V.L.'s mother kept a tidy home. Although her children's clothes were hand-me-downs, each garment showed the signs of loving care. Every pair of pants and every dress was clean, mended, and pressed. To this day, it makes V.L. chuckle when he remembers a long line of shared clothing: "The first kid up on Sunday morning was always the best dressed one at church."

In 1935, while the Depression was in full swing, V.L. was given the opportunity of a lifetime. He had always been good at sports—taking solace in the distraction of a game, its passion, and working as part of a team. His talent for football shone so brightly that it attracted the attention of Mississippi College. V.L. had a chance to make something better of his life, to be more than a sharecropper. V.L. had a way out.

With bags packed, he said his good-byes, hugged his family, and headed off toward a brighter future. But memories of home were never far behind. V.L. worried about his loved ones on the farm. Without his help, how would they make it? Maybe college wasn't for him. He was needed back home; that's where he truly belonged.

Within a year, V.L. signed himself out of school and headed for home, back to his family, back to life on the farm. For many, his decision was foolish. He was giving up a chance, a future so promising, and for what—working on someone else's land? But V.L. was determined. He knew it was the right thing to do. What good would success be if he left others behind? He would struggle with them, and, in time, God would see them through.

Years went by, and V.L. never doubted his decision. Soon the Depression ended, the economy began to improve, and now, with work done, he headed out for greener pastures. V.L. held many jobs over the years. He labored in factories and even managed a few honky-tonks.

In time, he was rewarded for his sacrifice. Little by little, he used what he'd learned as a child. He bought land in Tennessee and began a produce business several states wide—the best beans, cabbage, and tomatoes around.

Today he shares that dream with his two sons and a daughter. Like their father, they have learned it takes teamwork to make a business prosper. But before they could join the venture, each was sent to college to get a degree. His children would have the opportunities he did not. V.L. saw to that.

God was watching when this benevolent man gave up an education, a future, to help his family back home, and God returned the blessing manyfold. V.L. now possesses land far and wide and has a thriving produce business to call his own. Surely, in time, he reaped what he sowed: great personal rewards in exchange for a giving heart.

An Angel to Guide Them

*I*t was 1999, and the popular band The Backstreet Boys had struck a chord in many young girls' hearts. Teri's daughters, Shelbie, 14, and Kristen, 12, were huge fans of the group. They sang along to the radio, hung posters on their walls, and begged their mom to take them to hear the band live in concert. Teri promised that if the group booked close to town, she'd take them, rain or shine. One afternoon, with excitement in their voices, the girls told her the news. They'd heard it on the radio: a concert was scheduled at an auditorium just a few hours away, near San Francisco. Could they please go? Good to her word, Teri purchased tickets, and before she knew it, they were on their way.

They sat in the center of an enormous crowd—young girls screaming and singing along and music that Teri admits was sweet. She was glad she could give her daughters a special moment to remember, an evening at a teenybopper concert with their mom.

When the last song ended, they struggled through the crowd and back to their car. Teri kissed her girls, buckled them up, and headed out of the parking lot. It was late, and they had a two-hour drive before them. Exhausted, she navigated toward the freeway, but it was so dark she became disoriented. Around and around she traveled the streets, seeing every freeway entrance but the one she was looking for. She tried not to panic or alarm her daughters, yet she couldn't help but fret: "It's late, my husband will be worried, and this is such a big city. What if we run out of gas? Where can I find a safe place to ask for help?"

Teri drove for more than 45 minutes, then headed back for the auditorium. How would she ever get home? Just as tears of desperation began to well up in her eyes, Teri had an idea. She needed to pray. With a peace only faith can bring, she asked God to send an angel to guide them. No sooner had she uttered those words when a policeman drove up beside her. Excited to see someone she could trust, Teri asked him for help. The officer smiled and told her to follow him. He was on his way home, going in just that direction.

Teri trailed the light from the patrol car down the dark streets, turning here and turning there, until finally the officer escorted her onto the freeway. With a honk and a wave, she headed safely for home. While Shelbie and Kristen sang concert tunes from the backseat, Teri's heart was filled with gratitude: appreciation for two happy children, for answered prayer, and for an angel to guide their way.

A Christmas Miracle

A traditional Christmas. That's what David and Linda Almas celebrated. Fresh-baked cookies, frosted to perfection; hot chocolate; and a roaring fire to warm their hearts. In the corner of the room, a beautiful tree, shining brightly, lights twinkling in the night, ornaments reflecting the wonder of the season. But no matter how perfect their holiday presentation, there was always something missing. David and Linda desired to share this sacred celebration with children of their own. They wanted to behold sweet angels, adorned in red plaid pajamas, as they sat on their laps, listening to the true Christmas story, the miracle of Christ's birth.

The couple waited five years for their prayers to be answered. And in 1987, their son, Justin, was born with much fanfare. Relatives and friends came from far and wide to share in their miracle. He was David and Linda's first child, someone to share their lives with, someone to hold and to love. Surely, each day from now on would be filled with wonder.

Justin was the joy of his parents' hearts. Each year after his birth, Christmas brought new hope, new reasons to celebrate. They loved to share the miracle of the true meaning of Christmas. On the morning of December 25, David would hold Justin on his lap and read from the Bible:

The star in the sky, the angels on high, announcing to poor shepherds, that on this night, in the town of Bethlehem, a child was born, a child, which is Christ the Lord.

Although they rejoiced in their blessings, Linda and David longed for another baby. They wanted to experience the thrill of a tiny newborn once more and to see Justin grow up with a little brother or sister. Yet in spite of years of trying, they were unable to conceive.

Eventually the couple met with doctors and began fertility treatments. Although procedures were intrusive and brought negative side effects, Linda and David were willing to do whatever they must to receive their precious gift. During this time, Linda conceived, but the pregnancy ended in miscarriage. When they recovered from the crushing blow, they were led in a new direction. What about adoption?

In 1992, after completing extensive research and interviewing agencies, they chose an adoption facilitator whose philosophy was much like their own. Papers were filled out, and home inspections were done. At the request of the facilitator, David and Linda put together a written and pictorial biography. They presented themselves for who they were: a young, loving family of three, looking to share their hearts, their love, and their home with another child. Within three months, a 19-year-old girl from Idaho responded to their plea.

Excited, but afraid to get their hopes up, David and Linda proceeded with a bit of caution and heartfelt prayer. They asked for God's wisdom and blessing: "If this is the child for us, please make a way. Please give us our miracle."

In October, David and Linda drove from California to Idaho to meet with the young woman and her parents. The two families seemed to connect on a true and deep level. Everyone agreed — they were a match. Now it was just a matter of time. The baby was due in December, such a busy season. "How would the timing work out?" they wondered.

Soon, Thanksgiving was upon them. It was a festive time in their household, moments filled with anticipation. There were pies to bake, and baby furniture to buy, a turkey to prepare, a bonnet to behold. Although their hearts were filled with gratitude — for a healthy family, for a new child on the way, and for answered prayer — David and Linda held back just a little. So much was still uncertain. They'd heard the horror stories before, of couples so excited, so hopeful, only to have their lives come crashing down around them when a birth mother, at the last moment, changed her mind. It could happen, and they knew it. David and Linda wanted only the best for this child, their own family, and the young woman. With prayer and open hearts, David and Linda knew that God would work out His perfect plan.

On Christmas morning, as they finished opening presents with Justin, David said, "Now all we need is the phone call that the most precious gift has arrived." Just as if on cue, the telephone rang. The birth mother was in labor. Could they make it to the hospital in time for the delivery? It was a long drive, and it was snowing. They would do all they could; God would do the rest.

On the wings of prayer, David and Linda arrived in the middle of the night. They dashed through the parking lot to the back door, where a nurse was waiting just for them: "No, she hasn't delivered yet." In the stillness of the dark snowy night, with prayers from around the country being sent up to heaven, God performed another miracle, and little Amanda was born. She was perfect, just as they knew she would be.

The next day, when the time came for the baby to be released, Linda became concerned. Could the birth mother really give Amanda up? Would she change her mind? Prayers were offered for wisdom. Suddenly, a still, small voice seemed to speak to Linda's heart. She sensed that the birth mom might be unable to directly hand her the newborn, to take Amanda from her loving arms and place her into another's. With a knowing in her soul, she brought the tiny car seat to the young woman and offered it to her. With the snow gently falling and the dawn of a new day breaking, the birth mom put the newborn into the seat, quietly handed Amanda to her new family, and then turned and walked away without ever looking back—a selfless gift, a true offering of love.

Before they knew it, David, Linda, and little Amanda were back on the highway, on their way to Colorado, where grandparents, aunts, uncles, and cousins were anxiously awaiting to meet the newest little angel in the family. In their hearts, they carried a song, for a wonderful New Year and many brighter tomorrows.

To this day, the Almas family continues their Christmas tradition. Each December 25, when fresh-baked cookies are frosted to perfection and hot chocolate is served, David lights a roaring fire. Then, as the tree twinkles in the night, they call for two angels adorned in red plaid pajamas, hold them on their laps, and read from the Bible:

The star in the sky, the angels on high, announcing to poor shepherds, that on this night, in the town of Bethlehem, a child was born, a child, which is Christ the Lord.

When the story ends, a new one begins. As two precious children listen intently, the couple shares the miracle of another Christmas. They share the blessed day God answered their prayers, the day He offered them little Amanda, the gift that's brought joy to their hearts, not just for a season, but for a lifetime.

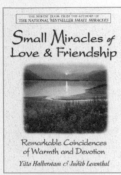